REASONING AND PROBLEM SOLVING

A HANDBOOK FOR ELEMENTARY SCHOOL TEACHERS

Stephen Krulik

Jesse A. Rudnick

Temple University

Allyn and Bacon

Boston   London   Toronto   Sydney   Tokyo   Singapore

Education Curriculum

Library of Congress Cataloging-in-Publication Data

Krulik, Stephen.
    Reasoning and problem solving : a handbook for elementary school
teachers / Stephen Krulik, Jesse A. Rudnick.
        p.   cm.
    Includes bibliographical references.
    ISBN 0–205–14006–8
    1.   Problem solving—Study and teaching.   2.   Mathematics—Study and
teaching (Elementary) I. Rudnick,   Jesse A.   II.   Title.
QA63.K776   1993
370.15—dc20   92–34069
                                                                          CIP

Printed in the United States of America

10 9 8 7 6 5 4 3 2 1   96 95 94 93 92

Contents

Preface

During the past decade, problem solving has emerged as the major priority in school mathematics. Indeed, one has only to compare any basal series of the 1990s with its counterpart from the early 1980s to realize the impact that problem solving has had on the mathematics classroom.

Now a new priority has emerged—teaching children to reason! This is a critical task for *all* teachers, but particularly for teachers of mathematics at all levels. A great many national publications have indicated how important these higher-order thinking skills appear to be. Reports such as *A Nation at Risk* (1983), *A Mathematics Report Card* (1988), and *Curriculum and Evaluation Standards for School Mathematics* (1989) have all emphasized the need for teaching higher-order thinking skills to our students along with problem solving. In this age of increasing dependence on technology and the increasing amount of information that must be processed daily, the power to reason, think, and problem-solve becomes more critical than ever before. No educator would deny the importance of teaching our students to think. But how should it be done?

We contend that these higher-order thinking skills should be developed through the teaching of problem solving, both as a topic of instruction and by the use of a problem-solving pedagogy throughout all teaching.

This book is designed to help you teach problem-solving and reasoning skills. Creative thinking, critical thinking, and problem solving are all aspects of student learning that must become part of our everyday teaching. We must make our classrooms reflect this desire for mathematical literacy and power for *all* our students. They must develop an appreciation for the power of mathematics, as well as the ability to appraise and evaluate quantitative data. Mathematical power must include the ability to "explore, conjecture and reason logically, as well as the ability to use a variety of mathematical methods effectively to solve non-routine problems" (*Curriculum and Evaluation Standards for School Mathematics*, 1989, p. 5). Reasoning skills and problem solving will be the major tasks facing mathematics teachers in the next decade.

We would like to acknowledge the dedicated educators who reviewed this manuscript and offered many valuable suggestions: Michele Nahas of Windham, Connecticut; Steven P. Meiring, Mathematics Specialist in the Ohio Department of Education in Columbus, Ohio; and Fred Lowman of the Avon Middle School in Avon, Connecticut.

S.K. and J.R.

CHAPTER ONE

An Introduction to Higher-Order Thinking Skills and Problem Solving

WHAT IS REASONING?

Currently in school mathematics, major emphasis is being placed on improving our students' ability to reason. But just what are these reasoning skills? Surely if we are to concentrate on this area of human activity, we must become knowledgeable about the subject. Many psychologists and researchers today are attempting to make a distinction between the terms "reasoning" and "thinking." During the day-to-day instruction of children, such a fine distinction is hardly necessary, but, as professionals, we should be aware of the difference. By thinking, we mean the ability of the child to reach a valid conclusion from a given set of data. The child must make conjectures, abstract properties from relationships in problem situations, then validate and explain his or her conclusions and assertions. These conclusions are then combined to form new ideas. In this book, we will consider *reasoning* to be a part of thinking that lies beyond the knowledge or recall level.

What are the thinking skills that include reasoning? The figure below shows the building blocks that form the hierarchy of thinking (Figure 1–1). We have divided thinking into four components: recall, basic, critical, and creative. Thinking is a complex process. Note that the categories shown are not discrete; each level makes extensive use of the skills contained in the levels that lie below it. In fact, within the higher-order thinking levels, there is a great deal of interaction, of moving back and forth.

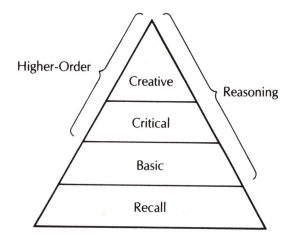

Hierarchy of Thinking

Figure 1–1

Recall

Recall thinking includes those thinking skills that are almost automatic or reflexive in nature. This might include the basic arithmetic facts — e.g., $3 \times 2 = 6$, $4 + 3 = 7$. These associations are made during the early years in school. In this early stage, students must make a conscious effort to commit these facts to memory. The ability to call up a basic fact or perform a given algorithm is *recall*. The material included in the recall block is constantly expanded as the individual progresses through the educational process. Thus, in mathematics such things as basic facts, computational algorithms, and percent occur early in the elementary grades. In the secondary grades, such things as

$$x = \frac{-b \pm \sqrt{b^2 - 4ac}}{2a}$$

(the quadratic formula), the Pythagorean Theorem, properties of common geometric shapes (e.g., the area of a circle = πr^2), and so on, are added to the recall/memory bank, to be called up as needed.

Basic

Basic thinking includes the understanding of mathematical concepts such as addition, subtraction, multiplication, and division, as well as the recognition of their application in problems, both in school and in everyday living. For example, if a child has to determine the cost of five ice cream cones at 75¢ each, recognizing that the multiplication concept is called for becomes fundamental to the solution. Note that recognizing the application of a particular operation does not necessarily imply an understanding of the concept. Thus an *understanding* of the concept of multiplication could be illustrated by showing that the product could have been obtained by adding 75¢ a total of five times, i.e., that multiplication is repeated addition.

Critical

Critical thinking is thinking that examines, relates, and evaluates all aspects of the situation or problem. This block includes such skills as *focusing* on the parts of the problem or confronted situation, *gathering* and *organizing* the information within the problem, *validating* and *analyzing* this information, and *remembering* and *associating* previously learned information. The ability to read with understanding is a critical skill, as is the differentiation between necessary and extraneous information. Recognizing what is being asked for or required is also a critical thinking skill. In a problem situation, recognizing that there is insufficient data or even contradictory data is a direct application of critical thinking. Determining the reasonableness of an answer that has been obtained also falls into this category of thinking. Critical thinking is analytical and reflexive in nature.

Creative

Creative thinking is thinking that is original, effective, and produces a complex product. Creative thinking is inventive, intuitive, and imaginative. This block includes such skills as synthesizing ideas, generating ideas, and applying ideas. By *synthesizing, ideas* we refer to different and unusual ways to combine information, and to elaborate on previous ideas. *Generating ideas* refers to formulating alternative approaches, forming new combinations from old ideas. *Applying ideas* means determining the effectiveness of the new ideas. Creative thinking is a continuum. Previous knowledge is synthesized, combined, and expanded to generate new ideas. These new ideas are then subjected to critical analysis and their effectiveness in resolving the problem situation is assessed. Further synthesis and generation then takes place, and the cycle continues. (See Figure 1–2.)

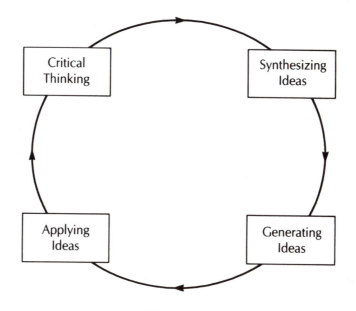

Figure 1–2

WHAT IS PROBLEM SOLVING?

Problem solving is a process. It is the means by which an individual uses previously acquired knowledge, skills, and understanding to satisfy the demands of an unfamiliar situation. The process begins with the initial confrontation and concludes when an answer has been obtained and considered with regard to the initial conditions. The student must synthesize what he or she has learned and apply it to the new situation.

WHAT IS A PROBLEM?

Fundamental to the problem-solving process are, of course, the problems that must be solved. A major difficulty in discussing problem solving is a lack of any clear-cut agreement as to what constitutes a "problem." A problem is a situation, quantitative or otherwise, that confronts an individual or group of individuals, that requires resolution, and for which no path to the answer is known. The key to the definition is the phrase "no path to the answer is known." As children pursue their mathematical training, what were problems at an early age become exercises and are eventually reduced to mere questions. We distinguish between the three commonly used terms as follows:

(a) *question*: a situation that can be resolved by recall from memory
(b) *exercise*: a situation that involves drill and practice to reinforce previously learned skills or algorithms
(c) *problem*: a situation that requires thought and synthesis of previously learned knowledge to resolve

In addition, a problem must be perceived as such by the student, regardless of the reason. If the student refuses to accept the challenge, then at that time, it is not a problem for that student. Thus a problem must satisfy the following three criteria, illustrated in Figure 1–3.

Acceptance   Blockage   Exploration

Figure 1–3

1. *Acceptance*:   The individual accepts the problem. There is a personal involvement, which may be due to any of a variety of reasons, including internal motivation, external motivation (peer, parent, and/or teacher pressure), or simply the desire to experience the enjoyment of solving a problem.
2. *Blockage*:   The individual's initial attempts at solution are fruitless. His or her habitual responses and patterns of attack do not work.
3. *Exploration*:   The personal involvement identified in (1) forces the individual to explore new methods of attack.

The existence of a problem implies that the individual is confronted by something he or she does not recognize, and to which he or she cannot merely apply a model. A situation is not considered a problem when it can be solved by merely applying algorithms that have been previously learned when the situation is like one previously encountered.

A word about textbook problems

Although most mathematics textbooks contain sections labeled "word problems," many of these "problems" should not really be considered as problems. In many cases, a model solution has already been presented in class by the teacher. The student merely applies this model to the series of similar exercises in order to solve them. Essentially the student is practicing an algorithm, a technique that applies to a single class of "problems" and that guarantees success if mechanical errors are avoided. Few of these so-called problems require reasoning by the students. Yet the first time a student sees these "word problems," they could be problems for him or her, if presented in a non-algorithmic fashion. In many cases, the very placement of these exercises prevents them from being real problems, since they either follow an algorithmic development designed specifically for their solution, or they are headed by such titles as "Word Problems: Practice in Division by 4."

We consider these word problems to be exercises or routine problems. This is not to say that we advocate removing them from the textbooks. They do serve a purpose, and for this purpose they should be retained. They provide exposure to problem situations, practice in the use of the algorithm, and drill in associated mathematical processes. A teacher should not think that students who have been solving these exercises through the use of a carefully developed model or algorithm are learning to become problem solvers. However, creative teachers by their approach can utilize these to help develop problem-solving skills.

WHY TEACH REASONING AND PROBLEM SOLVING?

"Every year nearly 1.5 million American 17-year-olds near the end of high school without much–needed mathematical reasoning skills. Fully a third of our 13-year-olds haven't mastered skills universally taught in elementary school. Few youngsters can put mathematics to work effectively in solving everyday problems, and some practical activity is absent from most classrooms."

This devastating indictment of school mathematics programs, which appeared in *The Mathematics Report Card*, published by Educational Testing Service in June 1988, highlights the need for a major effort to improve the reasoning and problem-solving skills of all of our students. Where is the natural place to begin this effort? In the elementary school! The mathematics program provides the ideal content area. This is not to say that other disciplines should not engage in the development of problem-solving and reasoning skills. Indeed, this should be the primary focus of the entire curriculum.

Even without the negative findings of this report, a strong case could be made for emphasis on problem-solving and reasoning skills. Research has shown that when thinking skills are taught directly, academic achievement increases. Problem solving and reasoning are fundamental to everyday life. All of our students will face problems, quantitative or otherwise, every day of their lives. Rarely, if ever, can these problems be resolved by merely referring to an arithmetic fact or a previously learned algorithm without reasoning. The words "Add me!" or "Multiply me!" never appear in a store window. *Problem solving provides the link between facts, algorithms, and the real-life problem situations we all face.* For most people, mathematics *is* problem solving! And problem solving *is* reasoning!!

In spite of the obvious relationship between the mathematics of the classroom and the quantitative situations in life, we know that children of all ages see little connection between what happens in school and what happens in real life. An emphasis on problem solving and reasoning in the classroom can lessen the gap between the real world and the classroom world and thus set a positive mood in the classroom.

Also, in many mathematics classes, students do not see any connections between the various ideas taught during the year. Most regard each topic as a separate entity. Problem solving shows the interconnections between mathematical ideas. Problems are never solved in a vacuum, but are related in some way to something seen before, something learned earlier, or something to be learned at a later time. Thus, good problems can be used to review past mathematical ideas, as well as to sow the seeds for ideas to be presented at a future time.

Problem solving is more exciting, more challenging, and more interesting to children than barren exercises. If we examine student performance in the classroom, we recognize the obvious fact that success leads to persistence and continuation of a task; failure, on the other hand, leads to avoidance. It is this continuance that we constantly strive for in mathematics. The greater the involvement, the better the end product. Thus, a carefully selected sequence of problem-solving activities that yield success will stimulate students, leading them to a more positive attitude toward mathematics in general and problem solving in particular.

Finally, problem solving permits students to learn and to practice heuristic thinking. A careful selection of problems is a major vehicle by which we provide the development of problem-solving and reasoning skills so necessary in real life.

WHEN DO WE TEACH PROBLEM SOLVING?

Problem solving is a lifetime activity. The child encounters problem solving almost from birth. The baby reaches for a favorite toy, cries when uncomfortable or wanting attention. However, the formal teaching and learning of the problem-solving process begins as soon as the child enters school and continues throughout his or her entire school experience. The elementary school teacher has the responsibility for beginning this instruction and thus laying the foundation for building the child's capacity to deal successfully with his or her future problem-solving encounters.

Since the process of problem solving is a teachable skill, when do we teach it? What does it replace? Where does it fit into the day-to-day schedule?

Experiences in problem solving are always at hand. All other activities are subordinate. Thus, the teaching of problem solving should be continuous. Discussion of problems, proposed solutions, methods of attacking problems, etc., should be considered at all times. Think how poorly students would perform in other skill areas such as fractions, if they were taught these skills in one or two weeks of concentrated work and then the skills were never used again.

Naturally, there will be times when studies of algorithmic skills and drill and practice sessions will be called for. We insist that students be proficient in the basic computational skills. Problem solving is *not* a substitute for these computational skills. However, the time spent on learning and practicing these skills will permit the delay necessary for the incubation period required by many problems, which need time to "set." By allowing time between formal problem-solving sessions, you permit students to become familiar with the problem-solving process slowly and over a longer period of time. This is important, since the emphasis is on the process and not merely on obtaining an answer. The development of the process takes time!

Of course we do not advocate that direct instruction in problem solving replace all the skills being taught. Not at all! Rather, we feel that problem solving should be utilized to create a *need* for these skills and an understanding of the concepts underlying the skills.

WHEN DO WE TEACH REASONING?

All the time! Thinking is a lifetime activity. Reasoning underlies everything we do! Every conscious activity involves some form of reasoning. Everything a person does results from conclusions drawn from the reasoning process. Of course, this excludes simple recall, which is almost reflexive in nature. Yet even this resulted from reasoning at an earlier stage, prior to becoming mere recall. Thus, the development of reasoning skills must be the primary goal of every teacher in every classroom. Teachers must take every opportunity in a classroom situation to encourage reasoning by students.

Even when we apply a specific skill such as the multiplication algorithm, thinking must take place. The recognition that multiplication is called for, the estimation of the answer preceding the application of the algorithm, and the comparing of the answer obtained by the algorithm to the estimation are all examples of reasoning that should be carried out along with the algorithm. Although reasoning should be a part of virtually every classroom activity, it is problem solving that provides a magnificent vehicle by which we can specifically help children develop their reasoning skills.

WHAT MAKES A GOOD PROBLEM?

Problem solving and reasoning are the basic skills of mathematics education. These are the primary reasons for including mathematics in the school curriculum. In order to teach these skills, teachers must have a resource bank of good problems. We need good problems to teach problem solving. A good problem for instructional purposes contains one or more of the following characteristics:

1. It is interesting and challenging to students.
2. It requires critical analysis and observation skills.
3. It provides an opportunity for discussion and interaction.

4. It involves the understanding of a mathematical concept and the application of a mathematical skill.
5. It should lead to a mathematical principle and/or generalization.
6. It lends itself to a variety of solutions and, at times, to multiple answers.

In this section, we will illustrate each of these characteristics with examples appropriate to the classroom. A more detailed discussion will occur in the chapter on how to teach problem solving and reasoning.

1. The problem is interesting and challenging to students.

A child's world differs significantly from that of an adult. Problems that would normally interest adults, such as some real-life applications, may be of no interest to children. Therefore, the problem setting and the action must center on the child's world. Teachers must be familiar with the child's world in order to select problems that are both interesting and appealing.

PROBLEM   Janice has fewer than 10 baseball cards. If she puts them into piles of 3, she has none left over. When she puts them into piles of 4, there is 1 left over. How many baseball cards does Janice have?

Discussion   Children enjoy collecting. Baseball is a sport that interests most of them. Thus, it is likely that a problem such as this one will appeal to most children.
The first two facts tell us that Janice has 3, 6, or 9 cards. The final fact tells us that the answer must be 9.

Notice that this problem exhibits several characteristics of a good problem. First of all, the mathematical content centers on the concept of division with remainders. Second, the problem can be extended by increasing the number of cards in the collection and/or by changing the number of cards in each arrangement. Third, it lends itself to more than one method of solution. That is, it can actually be acted out by using cards or other manipulatives. It can also be done abstractly with paper and pencil, or it can be done mentally by guessing at an answer and then testing the guess. Finally, as we have already stated, collecting baseball cards is within the realm of the child's experience and is of interest to most children.

PROBLEM   Giraffes walk in an unusual manner. On one step, they move their 2 right feet. On the next step, they move their 2 left feet. Then they move their 2 right feet and so on. If a giraffe takes its first step with its 2 right feet, which feet will it move on the seventh step? Explain how you would decide which feet the giraffe moves on any step.

Discussion   Most animal activities are interesting to children. This attribute of the giraffe, which is shared by some horses (pacers), is not only interesting and challenging, but also provides us with an opportunity to expose the children to simulation and listing. It also brings up the mathematical concept of even and odd. The second question places the child in a reasoning environment, one that requires creative thinking, generalization, and communication.

2. The problem requires critical analysis and observation skills.

PROBLEM   In Figure 1–4, which doesn't belong?

Figure 1–4

Discussion   This non-verbal problem requires the student to determine the characteristics common to 3 objects but not to the fourth. In this case, the baseball, basketball, and bowling ball are all round; the football is oval. Thus, the football does not belong. Some students may decide, however, that the bowling ball does not belong, since it is made from a synthetic (non-leather) material, is the only one without any stitching or lacing, and is the only one with holes in it. Some students may arrive at their answer by using a different reason. In fact, some may arrive at a different answer entirely. This is an important fact: *Answers can vary!* In life, there are times when several answers can serve or be acceptable. The same should be true in our classroom problems. A discussion of all of the answers by the students is vital to the teaching of problem solving and reasoning.

PROBLEM   How many beads are on the string in Figure 1–5?

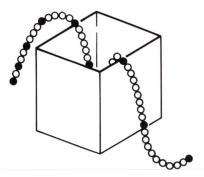

Figure 1–5

Discussion   The problem requires the student to observe the increasing number of white beads separated by a black one. Thus, there are really 2 sets of beads to be considered. The number of white beads can be found by summing the series $1 + 2 + 3 + \cdots + 8 + 9$. The 6-bead and 7-bead segments are hidden inside the box and must be determined by analyzing the sequence. The 10 black beads are determined by recognizing that they represent the endpoints of 9 intervals. Thus, there are 55 beads in all.

3. The problem provides an opportunity for discussion and interaction.

Problem solving goes beyond simply finding an answer. The classroom setting should provide an opportunity for students to talk with each other as they solve the problem. They should question each other's approaches and discuss the answer or answers arrived at. Students must be able to explain and defend their solution procedures to the rest of the class. Open-ended problems are an excellent way for teachers to generate this kind of reasoning.

PROBLEM   Supply the next two terms in the sequence 2, 4, 6.

Discussion   The initial reaction from most students would be 8 and 10. Further discussion will lead to other possible answers such as:

2, 4, 6, <u>10</u>, <u>16</u>   (obtained by adding the two previous terms)
2, 4, 6, <u>2</u>, <u>4</u>   (obtained by repeating the sequence)
2, 4, 6, <u>4</u>, <u>2</u>   (obtained by the use of symmetry)
2, 4, 6, <u>12</u>, <u>14</u>   (obtained by adding 10)

and so on.

PROBLEM   Janie went to the SUPERMAC and spent $3. (See Figure 1–6) What did she buy?

SUPERMAC MENU	
Superburger	$1.50
Superburger with cheese	$1.60
Big Chick (grilled) Special	$1.25
French fries	
Large	.75
Medium	.50
Drinks	
Coffee	.50
Iced tea	.50
Cola	
Large	.85
Medium	.80
Small	.75

Figure 1–6

Discussion   Problem of this type should be solved by small groups of students working together. Cooperative learning is a prime method for developing interactive and communicative skills. Problems such as this, for which there are many correct answers, should be an ongoing part of the problem-solving experience. Notice that there are many ways Janie might have spent her $3. For example, she might have bought 6 medium french fries; or 2 superburgers; or 1 Big Chick, one small cola and 2 medium fries. Each group of students should present its answer(s) and explain how it was reached.

PROBLEM   The Carpenter family called up to order a pizza while they were watching the football game. "Cut it into 4 pieces," said Rusty, "and put mushrooms on all of it." "I want broccoli on half of it," said Mrs. Carpenter. "I want olives on half," said Mr. Carpenter. "And I want pepperoni on half, but not with the broccoli," said Susan. When the pizza arrived, all family members agreed that it was just what they had ordered. How were the toppings arranged on the pizza?

Discussion   At first, this problem appears to be impossible, since 4 different toppings are required to be placed on 3 halves of the same pizza. The students should discuss where the toppings should go, and how a drawing of the pizza would help solve the problem. One possible answer:

Mushroom Broccoli Olives	Mushroom Broccoli
Mushrooms Olives Pepperoni	Mushrooms Pepperoni

PROBLEM   The hands on the clock in Figure 1–7 are both the same size. How can you tell what time the clock really shows?

Figure 1–7

Discussion   The problem will naturally create a discussion. More observant children will note that at 11:45, the "small" hand would not be exactly on the 12. Other students might suggest waiting 5 minutes to see what happens as the hands move.

4. The solution to the problem involves the understanding of a mathematical concept or the application of a mathematical skill.

Many problems appear, on the surface, to be non-mathematical yet their solution involves basic mathematical principles or concepts. Recognition of an appropriate skill and its proper applications may quickly resolve the problem. In any case, there should be some basic mathematical skill and/or concept embedded in the problem and its solution.

PROBLEM   There are 30 children in line to ride the ferris wheel at the local fair. Each car carries exactly 4 children. Jorge and Perry are number 17 and 18 in line. Will they ride in the same car?

Discussion   To solve this problem we can make a table:

Student Number	Car Number
1, 2, 3, 4	1
5, 6, 7, 8	2
9, 10, 11, 12	3
13, 14, 15, 16	4
17, 18, 19, 20	5

Yes, Jorge and Perry will both ride in car number five.
A table is not necessary if the child understands the concept of division and interpreting remainders. Divide 4 into 17 and then into 18. In each case, we get 4 and a remainder. Thus, 4 cars go before, and children 17 and 18 are in the next car, number 5. The child should also recognize the last figure in each row of the Student Number column and the figure immediately following in the Car Number column represent the multiplication table for 4.

PROBLEM   The new store in the mall opened last Saturday. As a promotional stunt, the store manager is giving a prize to every boy-girl pair that enters the store. Al, Benji, Charlie, Donna, and Evelyn are standing outside the store. Al turned to the others and said, "I wonder how many prizes we can get!" Donna answered, "If we do it carefully, we can get 6 prizes!"
Was Donna right? What was her thinking? How could they do it?

Discussion   One solution to this problem involves an application of a fundamental mathematical concept known as the counting principle. If there are 3 boys and 2 girls, then there are 3×2 or 6 different couples. The solution to the problem can be made more visible by using a tree diagram to obtain the boy-girl combinations.

PROBLEM   Mimi is older than Susan. Nancy is older than Mimi. Who is the youngest of the 3 girls?

Discussion   The solution to this problem depends on an understanding of the order principle and the property of transivity. Some students may have to act out the problem in order to solve it, by choosing 3 classmates who fit the given conditions.

PROBLEM   The floor of the monkey house at the local zoo is in the shape of a square (6 feet by 6 feet) and covered with Astroturf. Next to this is the gorilla house. Here the floor is also a square, but each side is twice that of the monkey house. What is the ratio of floor space in the gorilla house to that of the monkey house?

Discussion   The floor of the monkey house requires 6 × 6 or 36 square feet of Astroturf. The floor of the gorilla house is 12 feet by 12 feet, or 144 square feet. Thus the ratio of the floors is 144:36, or 4:1.
This problem depends upon the concept of area as it relates to the square. Notice that this is a multi-stage problem, requiring the student first to find the area of each floor and then to compare them. Notice, too, that this problem lays the foundation for the later study of the relationship between changes in the dimensions of a figure and the change in area that results. The multiplying of the linear dimensions by k results in an area that has been multiplied by k^2.

PROBLEM   The new school has exactly 1,000 lockers and exactly 1,000 students. On the first day of school, the student meet outside the building and agree on the following plan: The first student will enter the school and open all of the lockers. The second student will then enter the school and close every locker with an even number (2, 4, 6, 8, . . .). The third student will then enter and "reverse" every third locker. That is, if the locker is closed, he will open it; if the locker is open, he will close it. The fourth student will reverse every fourth locker, and so on until all 1,000 students in turn have entered the building and reversed the proper lockers. Which lockers will finally remain open?

Discussion   It seems rather futile to attempt this experiment with 1,000 lockers and 1,000 students, so let's take a look at 20 lockers and 20 students and try to find a pattern.
In our smaller illustration in Figure 1–8, the lockers with numbers 1, 4, 9, and 16 remain open (O) while all the others are closed (C). Thus, we conclude that those lockers with numbers that are perfect squares will remain open when the process has been completed by all 1,000 students. Notice that a locker "change" corresponds to a divisor of the locker number. An odd number of "changes" is required to leave a locker open. Which kinds of numbers have an odd number of divisors? Only the perfect squares!

17

Locker #	1	2	3	4	5	6	7	8	9	10	11	12	13	14	15	16	17	18	19	20
Student 1	O	O	O	O	O	O	O	O	O	O	O	O	O	O	O	O	O	O	O	O
2	▲	C	O	C	O	C	O	C	O	C	O	C	O	C	O	C	O	C	O	C
3			C	C	O	O	O	C	C	C	O	O	O	C	C	C	O	O	O	C
4				O	O	O	O	O	C	C	O	C	O	C	C	O	O	O	O	O
5				▲	C	O	O	O	C	O	O	C	O	C	O	O	O	O	O	C
6						C	O	O	C	O	O	O	O	C	O	O	O	C	O	C
7							C	O	C	O	O	O	O	O	O	O	O	C	O	C
8								C	C	O	O	O	O	O	O	C	O	C	O	C
9									O	O	O	O	O	O	O	C	O	O	O	C
10									▲	C	O	O	O	O	O	C	O	O	O	O
11											C	O	O	O	O	C	O	O	O	O
12												C	O	O	O	C	O	O	O	O
13													C	O	O	C	O	O	O	O
14														C	O	C	O	O	O	O
15															C	C	O	O	O	O
16																O	O	O	O	O
17																▲	C	O	O	O
18																		C	O	O
19																			C	O
20																				C

Figure 1–8

In summary, this problem has embedded in it several basic mathematical concepts, namely factors, divisors, composites, and perfect squares.

The problem also lends itself to an experiment, by having students act it out. Twenty students, each holding cards numbered from 1 through 20 represent the lockers. Having them turn facing forward (open) or facing backwards (closed) as they are "reversed" enables them to demonstrate the action described in the problem.

5. The problem should lead to a mathematical principle and/or generalization.

A problem is not necessarily finished when a satisfactory answer has been found. Rather, a deeper analysis of the solution will reveal the underlying mathematical principle and/or lead to a generalization.

PROBLEM   The score at the end of the eighth inning of the championship baseball game was 8–8. How many different scores were possible at the end of the seventh inning?

Discussion   Since 8–8 offers a great many possibilities, a good strategy to use to solve the problem would be reduction and expansion. Begin with 0–0, then 1–1, 2–2, and so on, keeping track of your results by means of a table similar to the one shown in Figure 1–9.

Score	Possible Scores	Number of
0–0	0–0	1
1–1	0–0 1–0 0–1 1–1	4
2–2	0–0 1–0 2–0 0–1 1–1 2–1 0–2 1–2 2–2	9
3–3	0–0 1–0 2–0 3–0 0–1 1–1 2–1 3–1 0–2 1–2 2–2 3–2 0–3 1–3 2–3 3–3	16
.	.	.
.		.
.		.
8–8		81
.		.
.		.
.		.
$m - m$		$(m + 1)^2$

Figure 1–9

Thus, the answer to this specific problem is 81 possible scores. Of course, if one considers the general case of a score of m to m, the result is shown on the table as $(m + 1)(m + 1)$ or $(m + 1)^2$.

How many scores would be possible if the score at the end of the eighth inning had been m to p, rather than a tie score?

PROBLEM   A set of children's blocks comes in 2 shapes: triangles and circles. Each shape comes in red, yellow, and blue. The blocks are thick or thin. How many blocks are in the set?

Discussion   The solution to this problem again utilizes the fundamental counting principle. Thus there are

2 (shapes) × 3 (colors) × 2 (thicknesses) = 12 blocks

This can be generalized to a (shapes) $\times$ b (colors) $\times$ c (thickness) and so on, to find the number of pieces in any set of blocks.

PROBLEM

Louise is having a party. At lunch, they are seated around a circular table. A platter of 25 sandwiches is passed around the table, with each person taking 1 sandwich from the platter and then passing it on to the next person. Louise takes the first sandwich and the last sandwich. How many people are seated at the table?

Discussion

The most apparent answer is that there are 24 people at the table, since Louise takes sandwich number 1 and sandwich number 25. However, there might also have been 6 people, and Louise takes sandwiches #1, #7, #13, #19, and #25. Similarly, there might have been 2 people, 3 people, 4 people, etc. In fact, all of the factors of 24 are possible for the number of people at the table.

This generalizes to the factors of (n-1) people, where n sandwiches are passed around and the first person takes sandwich number 1 and sandwich number n (and possibly others in between). What happens if (n-1) is a prime number such as 11?

PROBLEM

Mrs. Saunders brings a pizza to class. She decides to cut it with 7 straight cuts, each a diameter of the circular pizza. How many pieces will result?

Discussion

A series of drawings will reveal that 1 cut produces 2 pieces; 2 cuts produce 4 pieces; 3 cuts produce 6 pieces, and so on. Thus, 7 cuts will produce 14 pieces.

This leads to the generalization that the number of pieces is twice the number of cuts; i.e., $2n$ pieces when n is the number of cuts.

How could Mrs. Saunders get an odd number of pieces? (This is impossible, since $2n$ is an even number for all integral values of n.)

6. The problem lends itself to a variety of solutions and, at times, to multiple answers.

Most problems can be solved by more than one method. A single problem can often be acted out; can be reduced to a simple arithmetic, algebraic, or geometric relationship; can be resolved with a drawing; or can be resolved by an application of logical reasoning.

Children should be encouraged to think creatively and to find alternate ways to solve the problem. Not only is this highly desirable for the development of creative thinking skills, but it increases children's problem-solving capabilities when they can solve a problem in several ways, rather than in just one. Thus the teaching of problem solving can help the student develop greater creative thinking skills.

Traditionally in mathematics classes, we have chosen problems that have unique answers. Children should also be exposed to problems that not only can be solved in several different ways, but also to problems that have multiple answers. Analyzing the conditions that led to the multiplicity of answers (each of which is correct), is an excellent experience for children to undergo critical thinking.

PROBLEM   A farmer has some pigs and some chickens. He finds that together they have 70 heads and 200 legs. How many pigs and how many chickens does he have?

Discussion 1   A series of successive approximations together with a table to record the data will enable students to solve the problem, as shown in Figure 1–10.

CHICKENS		PIGS		TOTAL		
Number of heads	Number of legs	Number of heads	Number of legs	Number of heads	Number of legs	
70	140	0	0	70	140	(Not enough legs)
50	100	20	80	70	180	(Still not enough legs)
40	80	30	120	70	200	

Figure 1–10

Discussion 2   We can reduce the problem's complexity by dividing by 10. Thus, we now have 7 heads and 20 legs. (When the answer has been obtained, we must remember to multiply by 10.) Draw 7 circles to represent the 7 animals (7 heads tells us that there are 7 animals) and attach 2 legs to each. This accounts for 14 legs (see Figure 1–11).

Figure 1–11

We must now distribute the remaining 6 legs. Affix 2 additional legs to each of the first 3 animals, as in Figure 1–12. This shows us that there are 3 "pigs" and 4 "chickens." The final answer, then, is 30 pigs and 40 chickens.

Figure 1–12

Discussion 3

Use the idea of a one-to-one correspondence. All chickens stand on 1 leg, all pigs stand on their hind legs. Thus, the farmer will see 70 heads and 100 legs. The extra 30 legs must belong to the pigs, since the chickens have 1 leg per head. Thus there are 30 pigs and 40 chickens.

PROBLEM

There are 20 children taking a hike through the Alaskan hills. They are walking single file through a pass. Two giant mosquitos at the other end have decided how they will bite the children. The first mosquito said, "I'll begin with the first one and then bite every third child (i.e., 1, 4, 7, 10, . . .)." The second mosquito said, "I'll begin with the second one and bite every other child (i.e., 2, 4, 6, . . .)." Which children get bitten twice? Which children don't get bitten at all?

Discussion 1

Act it out! Select 20 children to stand in a straight line. Have two "mosquitos" give a card to each child they "bite." See who has 2 cards, 0 cards.

Discussion 2

Make an organized list:

Mosquito #1	Mosquito #2
1	2
4	4
7	6
10	8
13	10
16	12
19	14
	16
	18
	20

It would be interesting for the children to discuss how many children would have to be in line for the next person to be bitten twice.

Discussion 3 Use manipulatives. Place a set of numbered cards from 1 through 20 on a desk. Place a red chip on the cards "bitten" by mosquito number 1, and a blue chip on those cards "bitten" by mosquito number 2. Which cards have 2 chips? No chips?

PROBLEM A rectangular field is enclosed by a fence that is 32 feet in length. Each side of the rectangle is a whole number of feet. What is the area of the enclosed field?

Discussion A rectangle field whose perimeter is 32 feet can have many sets of dimensions—1 × 15, 2 × 14, 3 × 13, . . . , 8 × 8. All of these are different, yet all are correct.

The Heuristics
of Reasoning
and Problem Solving

WHAT ARE HEURISTICS ?

Both problem solving and reasoning are process skills—processes that start when the initial encounter is made and end when the obtained answer is reviewed in light of the given information. Children must learn these processes if they are to deal successfully with the problem situations they will meet in school and in other parts of life. Each *process* consists of a series of mental and physical tasks, loosely linked together to form what is called a set of *heuristics* or a heuristic pattern. These are a set of suggestions and questions that students must follow and ask themselves in order to resolve their dilemmas.

Heuristics should not be confused with algorithms. Algorithms, normally presented to children in classrooms, are schemata that are applied to a single class of problems. In computer language, they are programs that can be called up to solve specific problems or classes of problems for which they were developed. For each problem or class of problems, there is a specific algorithm. If one chooses and properly applies the appropriate algorithms and makes no arithmetic of mechanical errors, the correct answer will be obtained. In contrast, heuristics are general and are applicable to all classes of problems. They provide the direction needed by all people to approach, understand, and resolve problems that confront them.

There is no single set of heuristics for problem solving or for reasoning. Several people have put forth workable models, and whether the student follows the ones put forth by Polya, Bloom, and others, or the one that appears in this book, is not important; what is important is that our students learn some set of carefully developed heuristics and that they develop the habit of applying them.

It is apparent that simply providing students with a set of heuristics to follow would be of little value. There is quite a difference between understanding the process on an intellectual plane (recognizing and describing it) and being able to apply the process. Thus, we must do more than merely hand the heuristics to the students. Instruction must focus on each stage of the process and the interrelationships between these stages. The goal of our classroom instruction is to have children develop these processes!

THE HEURISTICS OF REASONING

A great deal is being written about the hierarchy and dimensions of thinking. A considerable amount of controversy exists between various definitions and taxonomies. However, we are concerned with helping classroom teachers to develop reasoning skills in their students. Thus, what follows is a workable heuristic plan that school-age children can follow, and some specific suggestions to teachers to assist them in their classroom instruction. Those knowledgeable about recent advances in the teaching of problem solving will recognize the similarity between the heuristics presented here and the heuristics of problem solving. We will deal with the latter in greater detail in the second part of this chapter.

Students cannot simply be told "Think!" Thinking does not take place without something to think about. Thus, the heuristics of reasoning will be applies to specific situations to which children can relate.

Figure 2–1 shows a workable set of heuristics that can form the basis of an instructional program in reasoning. This flow chart represents a continuum of thinking that every person should use when confronted by a situation that requires resolution. The categories are not discrete; a person who is resolving a situation moves back and forth between the categories. In fact, the more experienced the reasoner, the more automatic the back-and-forth motion becomes.

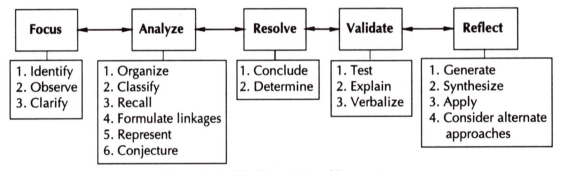

Figure 2–1   The Heuristics of Reasoning

Each of the five headings is expanded by the use of a set of descriptive subskills listed below it. The teacher has the responsibility for developing the heuristic process by creating situations in which students are involved in using these subskills.

1. Focus.

Focus goes beyond merely looking at the situation. In the initial stage, certain images are formed, including recognizing properties and characteristics, in order to get a feel for the situation. The question being asked then causes the person to focus more clearly on these relationships.

1a. Identify the task at hand.
1b. Observe the given material.
1c. Clarify attributes, properties, and terminology.

PROBLEM   In Figure 2–2, which of the lettered figures belongs with the other three?

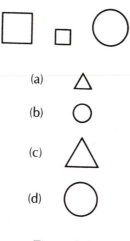

(a)

(b)

(c)

(d)

Figure 2–2

Discussion   What are you asked to do? What kind of figures are in the given material? What kinds of figures are in the set of possible choices? There are 2 squares and a circle in the given materials ; there are 2 triangles and 2 circles in the set of choices. What properties are involved other than just shape?

PROBLEM   In Figure 2–3, which doesn't belong?

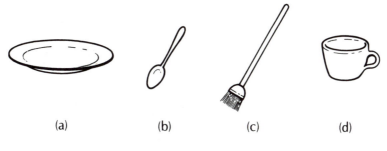

(a)   (b)   (c)   (d)

Figure 2–3

PROBLEM   Which doesn't belong?

(a) sled   (b) wagon   (c) automobile   (d) airplane

PROBLEM   Which doesn't belong?

2,   4,   7,   12

PROBLEM   Find three other numbers that belong with these:

4,   16,   36

Discussion   What are you asked to do? What are the given elements? What properties are there? What can you observe about each element?

PROBLEM   How could a person throw four darts and score a total of 12 points on the target shown in Figure 2–4 if each dart thrown sticks to the target?

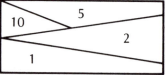

Figure 2–4

Discussion   What is the given task? What are you asked to do? How many darts will you throw? What scores are on the target? Could you score 12 in more than one way? What if one dart lands on a line? What happens if the first dart lands on the 10?

2. Analyze.

For thinking people, analysis takes place concurrently with focusing on the situation. In other words, it is impossible to separate these actions; the eyes and the mind are constantly interchanging information. However, we want our students to know that these are separate tasks undertaken within the thinking process, even though it is impossible to separate the actions clearly.

In this phase, we begin to examine our information. We compare, contrast, and classify the facts in order to make sense of the data. This requires proper organizational skills such as making a list, a table, or a drawing. It may involve making a mental note of similarities and/ or differences. These actions, along with recall of previous knowledge, should lead to a conjecture.

2a. Organize the information.
2b. Classify the data according to attributes.
2c. Recall appropriate information.
2d. Formulate linkages.
2e. Represent the data with appropriate symbols.
2f. Conjecture.

PROBLEM Supply the next word in the sequence: king, prince, father.

Discussion The task is to find the fourth word in the sequence. To do this, we organize the facts and look for relationships.

$$\downarrow \quad \begin{array}{ccc} \text{king} & \longrightarrow & \text{father} \\ \hline \text{prince} & \longrightarrow & \text{?} \end{array} \quad \downarrow$$

Notice that the ability of students to make a conjecture will depend upon their knowing the terms used in the situation.

PROBLEM Mary is preparing breakfast. Arrange the four actions in the order in which she should do them.

(a) Crack open 2 eggs into a mixing bowl
(b) Take 2 eggs from the refrigerator
(c) Take out a frying pan
(d) Pour the eggs into the frying pan.

Discussion Students must think in terms of a time-line. Organize the actions along the line:

$$\xrightarrow{\quad\quad (b) \quad (a) \quad (c) \quad (d) \quad\quad}$$

Could there be other arrangements?

PROBLEM The Johnson family has 5 members. Pair each family member with his or her name.

(a) Dan and Tom have a sister, Sue.
(b) Alice is Tom's mother.
(c) Ralph is married to Alice.

Discussion Students use recall to establish the relationships "mother," "father," "sister," "brother," etc. Linkages between names and family membership are tentatively established. You may illustrate representation in this problem by drawing a family tree.

PROBLEM   Find the next two terms in the sequence

1, 3, 6, 10, 15, ____, ____

Discussion   Help students recall experiences with patterns. Make conjectures as to the pattern rule.

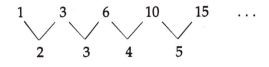

3. Resolve.

Once your students have observed and analyzed the situation, they should draw conclusions and determine the final answer.

3a. Draw final conclusions.
3b. Determine the answer.

PROBLEM   Draw the missing hands on the third clock in Figure 2–5.

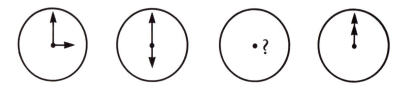

Figure 2–5

Discussion   Observing the drawings and analyzing the given times, students should be helped to see the sequence of hours. Mathematically the sequence can be represented as

3, 6, ____, 12

Students should conclude that the missing "time" is 9 o'clock, and draw the hands of the third clock to show that.

PROBLEM   The faces of the cube shown in Figure 2–6 are numbered in order. What is the sum of the numbers on all the faces?

Figure 2–6

Discussion Students will recall that there are six faces on a cube. They should observe that 26, 27, and 31 are shown. Analysis shows that three faces must still be identified, and that 28, 29, and 30 are missing from the sequence. The conclusion is that they are the missing numbers. Thus the sum is 171.

PROBLEM Three basketball players—Karl, Louis, and Marc—are all over 6'6" tall. A fan wants to know which one is the tallest. She knows that:

(1)   Marc is either the tallest or the shortest of the 3 players.
(2)   If Marc is taller than Karl, then Louis is the tallest.
(3)   If Louis is taller than Marc, then Karl is the tallest.

Discussion Carefully focusing on the problem at hand tells us that we must order the 3 basketball players according to their height. Linking statements (1) and (2) leads us to conclude that Marc is the shortest. Further analysis permits us to conclude that the order of height is Karl–Louis-Marc, from tallest to shortest.

4. Validate.

The activity is not really finished when a conclusion has been reached. The answer must be tested to determine its validity. Finally, the students should be encouraged to explain aloud how they reached their conclusion. This permits metacognition to take place and also helps to build communication skills.

4a. Test your conclusions.
4b. Explain how you know your conclusions are correct.
4c. Verbalize how he conclusion was obtained.

PROBLEM Figure 2–7 shows three views of the same cube. Determine which pair of faces are opposites.

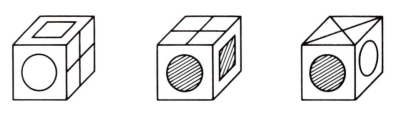

Figure 2–7

Discussion   Once the conclusion has been reached that the opposite faces are as shown in Figure 2–8, students must demonstrate that this is indeed correct.

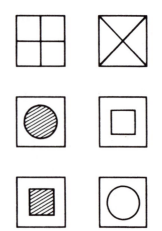

Figure 2–8

One way is to build a model of a cube with the faces as shown. An explanation should accompany this, demonstrating that the conditions have been met. At this point, the student should verbalize how their conclusions were reached. (For example, Why can't + be opposite the open circle or the open square ?)

PROBLEM   On Monday, Amanda gave away half of the records in her collection. On Tuesday, she gave away half of the remainder. Does she now have any records left?

Discussion   The answer is obviously "Yes !" The children should be able to explain that, in the second action, we are only taking half of the remaining one-half, which leaves one-fourth of the original collection. This explanation can take the form of a model, a drawing, or a verbal response.

PROBLEM   Michael ordered a 10-inch pizza. When the pizza came out of the oven, the baker asked Michael whether he wanted it cut into 6 pieces or 8 pieces, Michael responded, "You had better cut it into 6 pieces, because I'm not very hungry and probably couldn't eat 8 pieces." Was Michael's answer a good one?

Discussion   Students should be able to explain why $\frac{6}{6}$ and $\frac{8}{8}$ of the same circle represent the same amount.

PROBLEM   There are 33 children in Martha's class. On a trip to the zoo, they go in cars that each hold 5 children. How many cars do they need to bring all of the children to the zoo?

Discussion   The explanation should account for the fact that we cannot have a fractional part of a car. Thus $33 \div 5 = 6\frac{3}{5}$, requiring 7 cars.

5. Reflect.

Even after validating the answer and verbally explaining the procedures followed, there are things that can be done to extend the thinking process. Here is where students can engage in creative thinking.

    5a. Generate new problems.
    5b. Synthesize the findings.
    5c. Apply to other situations.
    5d. Discover alternative approaches.

PROBLEM   The faces of the cube shown in Figure 2–9 are numbered in order. What is the sum of the numbers on all faces?

Figure 2–9

Discussion   This problem has already been discussed. The missing faces contained the numbers 28, 29, and 30, and the answer to the problem was 171. Now we can generate a new problem by changing one of the numbers shown from 31 to 30. This new problem has *two* possible answers. The missing faces might contain 25, 28, and 29, (giving a sum of 165), or they might be 28, 29, and 31 (giving the sum of 171, as before). The new problem was generated by changing a condition of the original situation. We refer to this as a "What if" activity. Using the "What if" activity provides an excellent opportunity for students to exercise creative reasoning. The use of other "What if" possibilities, such as changing the shape of the figure or using other number combinations, gives additional experiences in creative thinking.

PROBLEM   An elephant ride at the zoo costs $3.00 for the first 10 minutes and 25¢ for each additional 5 minutes. Liam paid $4.00 for his elephant ride. How long did he ride?

Discussion   We can make a table to solve this problem:

Cost	$3.00	$3.25	$3.50	$3.75	$4.00
Number of Minutes	10	15	20	25	30

The table reveals that Liam rode for 30 minutes.

Now that an answer has been obtained and checked, a great deal can still be gained by finding an alternate solution—what we refer to as "Play it again!" This activity maintains the original conditions, but requires the student to find another solution. This particular problem can also be solved by working backwards:

$$
\begin{array}{rl}
\$4.00 & \longleftarrow \quad \text{total cost} \\
-\ \$3.00 & \longleftarrow \quad \text{first 10 minutes} \\
\hline
\$1.00 & \longleftarrow \quad \text{remainder of the ride}
\end{array}
$$

$1.00 ÷ .25 = 4. Liam took 4 additional 5-minute segments, or 20 minutes. Twenty minutes plus 10 minutes equals 30 minutes. Creative thinking is highlighted when the student is encouraged to "Play it again!"

APPLYING THE HEURISTICS

Now that each step of our heuristic model has been discussed, let's apply the model to several problems. As the solutions are developed, be certain that you are aware of the thinking processes that take place in each step.

PROBLEM In the Sunset Hockey League, a team gets 10 points for a win and 5 points for a tie. Teams also get 1 point for each goal they score. Last week, the Apes, Baboons, and Chimpanzees played each other once. There were no shutouts. The weekly totals were: Apes—20 points; Baboons—19 points; Chimpanzees—5 points. What were the scores of the games?

Discussion *1. Focus.*
Identify the task at hand. Observe the given material. Clarify attributes, properties and terminology.
We are asked to find the scores of all the games played. Observe the key facts : the Apes, Baboons, and Chimpanzees played each other once; the point totals were 20, 19, and 5 respectively. Teams receive 10 points for a win, 5 points for a tie, plus 1 point for each goal they score. There were no shutouts. Clarify the terminology: what is meant by a shutout? What is meant by a goal? Is 0-0 considered a shutout?

2. Analyze.
Organize the information. Classify the data. Recall appropriate information. Formulate linkages. Represent the data. Conjecture.
Make a table.

	Apes	Baboon	Chimpanzees
Game 1			
Game 2			
Game 3			

Recognize that 3 games were played: Apes–Baboons; Apes–Chimpanzees; Baboons–Chimpanzees. Reason that no team could have won 2 games; if a team had *won* 2 games, that team would have received 20 points without taking into account any goals. Similarly, the Chimpanzees could neither have won nor tied; their 5 points must have come from goals.

3. Resolve.
Draw final conclusions. Determine the answer .
The Apes and Baboons each receive 10 points for defeating the Chimpanzees. Since no team could win 2 games, the Apes and Baboon must have tied, each receiving 5 points. The Apes remaining 5 points came from goals, as did the remaining 4 points for the Baboons and the 5 points for the Chimpanzees. Guess and test reveals the scores to be:

Game 1	Apes 1, Baboons 1
Game 2	Apes 4, Chimpanzees 3
Game 3	Baboons 3, Chimpanzees 2

4. Validate.
Test your conclusions. Explain correctness. Verbalize process.
The Apes scored 10 points for their win over the Chimpanzees, 5 points for their tie with the Baboons. They scored 5 goals for a total of 20 points. Similarly, the Baboons scored 10 points for their win over the Chimpanzees, 5 points for their tie with the Apes, and 4 goals for their 19 points. The Chimpanzees scored 5 goals for their 5 points.

5. Reflect.
Generate new problems. Synthesize findings. Apply to other situations. Discover alternative approaches.
What if shutouts were permitted? Would we have different scores for the 3 games? Are our original scores unique? Are there other possibilities? Could there be a different way to solve the problem?

PROBLEM

A group of 3 boys and 2 girls were walking through the local mall when they noticed a sign in the bookstore window. The sign said that a special gift would be given to any couple that visited a display inside the store. The group decided to take advantage of the promotion. What is the maximum number of special gifts they could receive?

Discussion

1. Focus.
Identify the task at hand. Observe the given material. Clarify attributes, properties, and terminology.
We are asked to find the maximum number of gifts the 5 children could receive. Observe the key facts: each different couple gets a gift. The children should realize that in this setting, a couple means 1 boy and 1 girl. There are 3 boys and 2 girls.

2. Analyze.
Organize the information. Classify the data. Recall appropriate information. Formulate linkages. Represent the data. Conjecture.

We can organize our data by labeling the boys as A, B, C and the girls as D and E. Arrange them in appropriate pairs (1 boy and 1 girl); keep track of the pairs so as not to duplicate or miss any.

3. Resolve.
Draw final conclusions. Determine the answer.
Make a list of all the possible couples.

$$A–D \quad A–E$$
$$B–D \quad B–E$$
$$C–D \quad C–E$$

Our list reveals 6 possible couples. The 5 children could receive as many as 6 gifts.

4. Validate.
Test your conclusions. Explain correctness. Verbalize process.
You can check your answer by doing the problem in another way. Bring 3 boys and 2 girls to the front of the room. Have them form different "couples" while the rest of the class keeps track. This experimental approach will produce the same answer: 6.

5. Reflect.
Generate new problems. Synthesize the findings. Apply to other situations. Discover alternative approaches.
This problem permits us to generate a whole group of new problems. What if a "couple" were defined as any 2 people regardless of sex? What if there were 4 boys and 3 girls?
Still another approach to the problem might be the use of manipulatives, such as colored chips being used to replace the youngsters. This problem could easily lead to the discovery of some simple combinatorial theory. If one action can occur in p different ways, followed by a second action that can occur in q different ways, then the 2 actions can take place together in $p \times q$ ways.

THE HEURISTICS OF PROBLEM SOLVING

Over the years, several heuristic plans have been developed to assist students in problem solving. For the most part, all of these are quite similar. We now put forth a set of heuristics that has proven to be successful with students and teachers at all levels of instruction:

1. Read and think
2. Explore and plan
3. Select a strategy
4. Find an answer
5. Reflect and extend

There represent a continuum of thought that every person should use when confronted by a problem-solving situation. The elements of this continuum are not discrete. As one is reading a problem and examining the relationships that exist, a plan is usually taking shape. As an outgrowth of this plan, a strategy is selected. An answer is found, and, in turn, is examined within the context of the original problem. Figure 2–10 shows the heuristic plan, with the subskills associated with each step:

1. Read and think.

As the student reads the problem, he or she should be interpreting the language, making connections, and recalling similar situations. A problem has an anatomy. It must contain facts and a question. It may also contain a setting and distractors. During this step in the process students should:

1a. Identify the facts.
1b. Identify the question..
1c. Visualize the situation.
1d. Describe the setting and visualize the action.
1e. Restate the problem in their own words.

The problems that follow can be used to assist children in attaining the subskills of the first heuristic, Read and think. For each of the problems, have the children discuss the items in 1a through 1e. Then solve the problem. This is the stage of the problem-solving process where critical thinking is highlighted.

PROBLEM Commemorative stamps are sold in sheets of 50 stamps. Mike bought 3 sheets of a new commemorative stamp. He put a block of 4 stamps from each sheet into his album, and the family used the rest to mail letters. How many stamps did the family use?

Discussion Describe the action in your own words. What is being asked? What facts are you given?

PROBLEM Mary and Joyce leave school at 3:00 P.M. and start toward home. Their homes are on the same street but lie in opposite

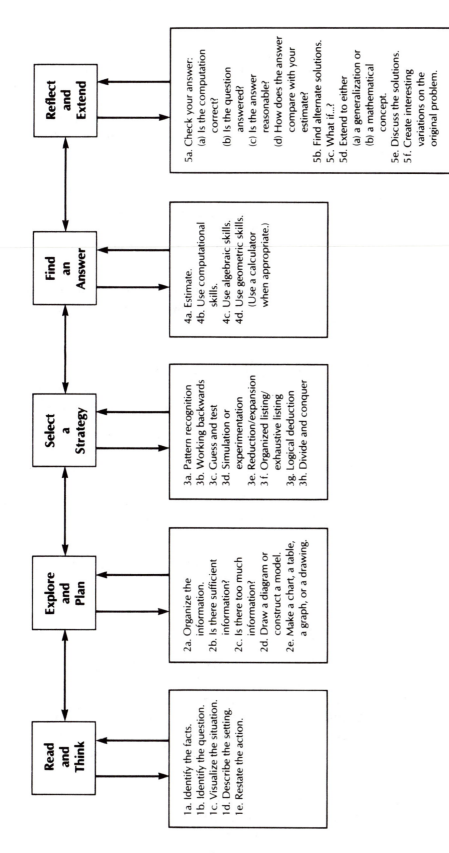

Read and Think

1a. Identify the facts.
1b. Identify the question.
1c. Visualize the situation.
1d. Describe the setting.
1e. Restate the action.

Explore and Plan

2a. Organize the information.
2b. Is there sufficient information?
2c. Is there too much information?
2d. Draw a diagram or construct a model.
2e. Make a chart, a table, a graph, or a drawing.

Select a Strategy

3a. Pattern recognition
3b. Working backwards
3c. Guess and test
3d. Simulation or experimentation
3e. Reduction/expansion
3f. Organized listing/ exhaustive listing
3g. Logical deduction
3h. Divide and conquer

Find an Answer

4a. Estimate.
4b. Use computational skills.
4c. Use algebraic skills.
4d. Use geometric skills. (Use a calculator when appropriate.)

Reflect and Extend

5a. Check your answer:
   (a) Is the computation correct?
   (b) Is the question answered?
   (c) Is the answer reasonable?
   (d) How does the answer compare with your estimate?
5b. Find alternate solutions.
5c. What if...?
5d. Extend to either
   (a) a generalization or
   (b) a mathematical concept.
5e. Discuss the solutions.
5f. Create interesting variations on the original problem.

Figure 2–10

41

directions from the school. Mary lives 3 miles from the school; Joyce lives 2 miles from the school. How far apart are their homes?

Discussion Can you visualize the action? Can you describe what is taking place? What question is being asked? What facts are given?

PROBLEM Mary and Joyce leave school at 3:00 P.M. and start toward home. Their homes are on the same street, and lie in the same direction from the school. Mary lives 3 miles from the school; Joyce lives 2 miles from the school. How far apart are their homes?

Discussion Can you visualize the action? Can you describe what is taking place? What makes this problem different from the preceding one?

PROBLEM Jeff weighs 160 pounds. His sister, Nancy, weighs 108 pounds. Their friend, Scott, weighs 26 pounds more than Nancy. What is the average weight of all three people?

Discussion Here, the important words are "more than", and "average." Words such as "more than, "less than," "subtracted from," etc. are often overlooked by students.

PROBLEM Mary is 12 years old and her bother George is 5 years older. How old is George?

Discussion The solution to this problem depends upon the child understanding the meaning of the word "older."

2. Explore and plan.

In this section of the heuristic plan, the problem solver analyzes and synthesizes the information contained in the problem that has been revealed during the previous stage. Here, many of these actions take place with little or no conscious thought. As students read the problem, ideas occur and plans take shape. Consciously, however, possible solutions are envisioned and mentally examined (hence the name Explore and plan.)

2a. Organize the information.
2b. Is there sufficient information?
2c. Is there too much information?

2d. Draw a diagram or construct a model.
2e. Make a chart, a table, a graph, or a drawing.

PROBLEM   A 5-pound bag of grapefruit contains 13 grapefruit. Find the difference between the number in the bag and a green basket that contains 1 dozen grapefruit.

Discussion   Notice that the 5-pound bag and the green basket are excess information. Also, there is no question mark, so what is the question being asked?

PROBLEM   At the ballpark, pizza costs 95¢ a slice, soft drinks cost $1.25, and a hot dog cost $2.05. Gladys bought a hot dog and a soft drink. How much change did she receive?

Discussion   This problem shows *both* excess information and insufficient data. The cost of the slice of pizza is excess, and the answer cannot be found because the amount of money given to the cashier is not known

PROBLEM   A log is to be cut into 5 equal pieces. How many times must the woodsman saw through the log?

Discussion   Students should draw a diagram as shown in Figure 2–11. The drawing reveals that the number of cuts is 1 less than the actual number of pieces required. Thus, the woodsman must saw through the log 4 times.

Figure 2–11

PROBLEM   Antelope Hill, Buffalo Corner, Coyote Canyon, and Desperado Gulch lie along a straight road in the order named. The distance from Antelope Hill to Desperado Gulch is 100 miles. The distance from Buffalo Corner to Coyote Canyon is 30 miles. The distance from Buffalo Corner to Desperado Gulch is 60 miles. How far is it from Antelope Hill to Buffalo Corner?

Discussion   Although the problem sounds cumbersome and complicated, it can be simplified by the use of a drawing like the one in Figure 2–12.

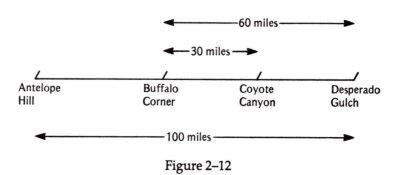

Figure 2–12

The key fact here is the phrase "in the order named." Notice that this makes the distance from Buffalo Corner to Coyote Canyon excess information.

PROBLEM   Last night, the Wolves played a basketball game against their crosstown rivals, the Foxes. Interestingly, there were no 3–point field goals scored by either team; all were 2–point field goals. For the Wolves, James scored 3 field goals and 2 free throws. Patrick scored 12 field goals and 5 free throws. Darryle scored 4 field goals and 6 free throws. Mel scored 5 field goals and 1 free throw. Liu scored 4 field goals and 4 free throws. In spite of these scores, the Wolves lost the game. How many points did the Foxes score?

Discussion   This problem illustrates the organization of data by the use of a table.

Name	Number of Field Goals	Field Goal Points	Foul Shots	Total Points
James	3	6	2	8
Patrick	12	24	5	29
Darryl	4	8	6	14
Mel	5	10	1	11
Liu	4	8	4	12
TOTALS	28	56	18	74

No exact score for the Foxes can be determined. However, the question can be answered by saying "More than 74 points." The "greater than" and "less than" relationships should be given consideration in problem solving.

PROBLEM   The fourth grade class planted 200 daffodils around the school building last fall. They planted half of them on the north side and half of what was left on the east side. Then they planted half of what was left on the south side, and all that remained on the west side. How many daffodils did they plant on each side?

Discussion   A drawing and\or a table as shown in Figure 2–13 helps the students to organize their data and solve the problem:

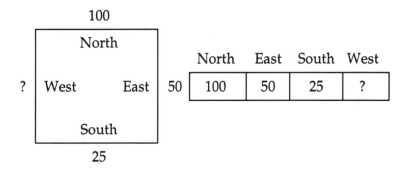

Figure 2–13

How is the number of daffodils planted on the west side determined?

3. Select a strategy.

As a result of the previous stages, the problem solver now must select the path that seems most appropriate. Below are eight identified strategies that are used most often, either independently or combined in some manner. Different people might approach a particular problem in different ways. A single problem can probably be solved by applying several combinations of these strategies. No one strategy is superior to any other, but some strategies may offer a more elegant path to the answer than others.

3a. Pattern recognition
3b. Working backwards
3c. Guess and test
3d. Simulation or experimentation
3e. Reduction/expansion
3f. Organized listing/exhaustive listing
3g. Logical deduction
3h. Divide and conquer

PROBLEM Find the next few terms in the sequence 1, 3, 5, . . .

Discussion The most obvious pattern is to continue the sequence of odd numbers. Thus the next few terms might be 7, 9, 11, ... However, some persons might think that the sequence only contains five terms and is symmetrical. Thus the entire sequence would be 1, 3, 5, 3, 1. A more sophisticated pattern rule might reveal 1, 3, 5, 17, 87, . . . ; i.e., $(a \times b) + 2$.

PROBLEM Find the next term in the sequence Ann, Brad, Carol . . .

Discussion Not all problems need be numerical. This sequence involves names. Note that this sequence contains 3 variables: alternation of gender, initial letters in alphabetical order, and increasing number of letters in each successive name. Thus the next terms might be Daniel and Eleanor. (How far can *you* carry the sequence?)

PROBLEM Amanda bought a strip of tickets at the carnival. She used one-third of her tickets on the Haunted House ride. Then she used half of what she had left to ride the swan boats. She used one-fourth of what she then had left to go on the ferris wheel. The remaining 15 tickets she gave to her cousin Allison. How many tickets did Amanda buy originally?

Discussion We solve this problem by working backwards and using logic. Allison received 15 tickets . This represented three-fourths of what Amanda had when she rode the ferris wheel (she had used one-fourth). This means that Amanda had 20 tickets then. The 20 was one-half of what she had before she went on the Swan Boats. Thus she had 40 tickets then, which represented two-thirds of what she bought. She must have bought 60 tickets.

PROBLEM   How many different ways can you add four even whole numbers and get 10 as the sum?

Discussion   Students should remember that "sum" implies addition. They should notice that they are to add four numbers, none of which can be an odd number. This problem is an excellent illustration of the use of the guess-and-test strategy. Students will try different sets of four numbers to see if they add up to 10. Keep guessing and checking until all the ways have been found. Keeping the results in an organized list will help. Notice that $4 + 2 + 2 + 2$ is the same as $2 + 2 + 2 + + 4$ is the same as $2 + 4 + 2 + 2$ and so on. These all count as one way.

PROBLEM   If you make a chain of paper clips, how many clips high is your desktop from the floor?

Discussion   This problem can be done by an experiment. Actually make a chain of paper clips, hold them from the floor to the top of the desk, and count! Answer will vary if the lengths of the individual paper clips are not the same. A more sophisticated solution might be to measure the height of the desktop in inches or centimeters, measure the length of 1 paper clip, and then divide the first figure by the second. Notice that this solution should provide practice in division of fractions. The answer to both of these approaches will probably be different. Why?

PROBLEM   Laura is training her white rabbit, Ghost, to climb a flight of 10 steps. Ghost can only hop up 1 or 2 steps each time he hops. He never hops down, only up. How many different ways can Ghost hop up the flight of 10 steps ?

Discussion   During the Read and Think stage, when the anatomy of a problem is discussed, students should learn that all of the numbers that appear in a problem are arbitrary decisions make by the person creating the problem. In some cases, 1 or more of these numbers can be modified without affecting the underlying problem, in order to simplify the solution. Children should learn which numbers can be modified and which must remain as they are. In this problem, the number of steps can easily be changed, but the pattern of 1 or 2 steps at a time cannot. Specifically, let's reduce the number of steps, given as 10, to 1, and expand to 2 steps, 3 steps, 4 steps, etc. and see if a pattern develops.

Number of Steps	Ways	Number of Ways
1	1	1
2	1-1,2	2
3	1-1-1 1-2 2-1	3

(Is this the sequence of the counting numbers? Don't be a conclusion jumper.)

4	1-1-1-1 1-1-2 1-2-1 2-1-1 2-2	5
5	1-1-1-1-1 2-2-1 2-1-1-1 2-1-2 1-2-1-1 1-2-2 1-1-2-1 1-1-1-2	8

The sequence 1, 2, 3, 5, 8 is familiar (a Fibonacci sequence). Thus, continuing the sequence, we obtain the answer:

$$1, \ 2, \ 3, \ 5, \ 8, \ 13, \ 21, \ 34, \ 55, \ 89$$

There are 89 different ways for Ghost to hop up the flight of 10 steps.

PROBLEM How many ways can Jeff make change for 50¢ without using pennies?

Discussion An organized list enables us to solve this problem:

Quarters	Dimes	Nickels
2	0	0
1	2	1
1	1	3
1	0	5
0	5	0
0	4	2
0	3	4
0	2	6
0	1	8
0	0	10

There are 10 different ways to make change.

Notice that in addition to being an organized list, this list is exhaustive. That is, *all* the possibilities have been listed. This solution is also an example of a simulation. We have simulated making change with a table.

PROBLEM   Mitchell just bought a new car. Les said it was a blue Dodge. Patricia said it was a black Chevrolet. Sandy said it was a black Ford. If each person correctly identified either the make of the car or its color but not both, what was the color and make of the car?

Discussion   Since each person identified correctly only 1 of the 2 attributes, a logical analysis reveals that the car must be black. Patricia and Sandy agreed on the color; if their color choice had been incorrect, the car would have to be both a Chevrolet and a Ford. Since this is impossible, the car is black. Since the car is black, Les was correct that the make is a Dodge.

PROBLEM   Michael Jordan scored four 3-point field goals, twelve 2-point field goals, and 7 free throws. How many points did he score?

Discussion   Divide the problem into its component parts and solve each part separately. The answer is then obtained by adding the results of these parts.

$$
\begin{aligned}
4 \times 3 \text{ points} &= 12 \text{ points} \\
12 \times 2 \text{ points} &= 24 \text{ points} \\
7 \times 1 \text{ point } &= 7 \text{ points} \\
\hline
\text{Total} \qquad &= 43 \text{ points}
\end{aligned}
$$

4. Find an answer.

Once the problem is understood and a strategy selected, students should estimate. This should result in a "ballpark" answer. Now the students should perform the mathematics necessary to obtain a more accurate answer. In most cases in the elementary grades, this mathematics consists of basic computational skills with whole numbers, decimals, and fractions, some metric properties of geometry, and some elementary algebra. A calculator should be used when appropriate.

4a. Estimate.
4b. Use computational skills.
4c. Use algebraic skills.
4d. Use geometric skills.

PROBLEM Mrs. Anderson bought five 6-packs of diet soda. Each can contains 12 ounces. How many ounces of soda did she buy?

Discussion The problem requires that the students understand the setting and the action. Multiplication is the required operation. This, however, is a two-stage problem that can be done in two different ways:

(a) $16 \times 12 = 72$ ounces per 6-pack
$72 \times 5 = 360$ ounces

(b) $6 \times 5 = 30$ cans of soda
$30 \times 12 = 360$ ounces

Notice that although the solutions differ somewhat, the answer is the same in both cases, as might be expected.

PROBLEM Gladys, Jeanette, Jesse, and Steve went fishing. Gladys caught 16 fish, Jeanette caught 13 fish, Jesse caught 17 fish, and Steve caught 14 fish. How many more fish did Jesse and Steve catch than Gladys and Jeanette?

Discussion The date in the problem can best be organized with a simple table:

Gladys	16
Jeanette	13
Jesse	17
Steve	14

Now we solve the problem by adding and then subtracting.

Jesse and Steve caught: $17 + 14 = 31$
Jeanette and Gladys caught: $16 + 13 = 29$

$$\begin{array}{r} 31 \\ -\ 29 \\ \hline 2 \end{array}$$

Jesse and Steve caught 2 more fish than Gladys and Jeanette.

PROBLEM At the amusement park, 18 people are waiting to go on a ride. A square car seats 4 people and a circular car seats 6 people. How can the people be seated in the cars?

Discussion   Students should use the guess-and-test strategy, keeping track of their guesses in a table. The problem involves a knowledge of the multiplication tables for 4 and 6.

Cars with 6	Cars with 4	Total Number
3	0	18
2	1	(16-less than 18)
1	3	18
0	4	(16-less than 18)

They can ride in 3 circular cars or in 1 circular and 3 square cars.

PROBLEM   Mary and Mike are each fencing in a garden in the shape of a rectangle with an integral number of units on each side. They each used 16 meters of fencing, yet Mary's garden contains 1 square meter more than Mike's. What were the dimensions of their gardens?

Discussion   The student must know about the area and perimeter of a rectangle. If the perimeter is 16, then the sum of one length and one width (the semiperimeter) would be 8. Several rectangles can now be drawn meeting the given conditions, as shown in Figure 2–14.

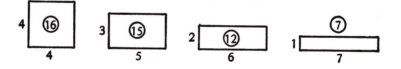

Figure 2–14

Thus, the drawing reveals that Mary's garden was really a square (4 × 4) and Mike's was a rectangle (5 × 3).

5. Reflect and Extend.

The "answer "is *not* the "solution." The solution is the process by which the answer is obtained. Therefore, once the answer has been arrived at, there is more to be done. This stage of the process consists of determining whether the question has been answered and the mathematics is correct, and how closely the answer agrees with the original estimate. Reflect on the process that was used, and discuss the various solutions with the class. Use "What if" questions to determine the relationships between the given facts and the answer . Create new problems that are interesting variations on the original. Finally, extend the problem to a generalization or a mathematical concept. This is the stage of the problem-solving process that requires the student to think creatively.

5a. Check your answer.
5b. Find alternate solutions.
5c. Ask "What if" questions.
5d. Extend the solutions, to generalizations and/or mathematical concepts.
5e. Discuss the solutions.
5f. Create interesting variations on the original problem.

PROBLEM   Find the length of 1 school desk if the sum of the lengths of 4 such desks is 20 feet.

Discussion   Notice that in this problem, the word "sum" does not ensure that the problem will be solved by addition.

$$20 \div 4 = 5$$

The answer appears to be 5 feet. Are the units correct? Does the method appear to yield the correct answer? Does the answer "make sense"? Why or why not ? What if the sum of the lengths of the 4 desks had been 22 feet ? Now how long would each desk be? If the sum of the lengths of the 4 desks had been 18 feet, would each desk be longer or shorter than in the original problem? Why?

PROBLEM   A farmer has 32 turkeys to send to market. He puts them into crates that each hold 4 turkeys when full. How many crates does he need if each crate must be full?

Discussion   The answer to this problem, obtained by recognizing the division concept, is obviously 8. Now, however, we can create new problems by asking a series of "What if" questions. What if the farmer had crates that held 4 turkeys or 5 turkeys? How many full crates would he need to ship the 32 turkeys to market?
Could he ship 7 turkeys? Why or why not?
What if he had an infinite number of turkeys to ship, and crates that hold either 5 turkeys or 4 turkeys? Could he ship

13 turkeys? Could he ship 9 turkeys? Could he ship 11 turkeys? Is there any number of turkeys, greater than 11, that he could not ship? What would it be?

The students should now discuss the various solutions that they develop.

PROBLEM   Ilsa threw 4 darts at the dartboard shown in Figure 2–15. They landed on 9, 5, 13, and 10. What was her score?

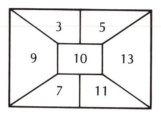

Figure 2–15

Discussion   As stated, this is merely a problem that requires simple addition. However, the problem lends itself to several interesting variations:

Ilsa hit the dartboard with 4 darts, and scored 45. How might she have done it?

What if the 10 were replaced on the target by a 15? Now how might Ilsa have scored her 45 with 4 darts?

Extend the problem to operations with even and odd numbers.

The usual practice in many textbook word problems has been to fine the answer, check it, and then go on to the next problem. However, it should be apparent that much more can be achieved toward the development of problem-solving ability if the conditions of the problem are altered and the resulting effect on the answer is examined. This provides the student with a much deeper insight into what has taken place in the problem-solving process. It also provides the opportunity for the student to develop the creative thought process.

APPLYING THE HEURISTICS

Now that each step of the heuristic process has been presented, discussed, and illustrated, let's apply the model to several problems. As the solutions are developed, be certain that you are aware of the thought processes being utilized in each step. Remember, problem solving is a *process;* the answer is merely the final outcome.

PROBLEM   Lorenzo is making a model of a Greek temple for a social studies project. He uses four square wooden blocks to make each column. To form an arch, he puts one block between the tops of two adjacent columns. How many blocks should he buy to make 12 arches?

Discussion   *1. Read and think.*
Describe the setting and visualize the action. What is being asked? What information is given?
The problem tells us that each column uses 4 blocks. An arch is created with two columns and 1 additional block. We are asked to find how many blocks are needed for the 12 arches?

2. Explore and plan.
Organize and represent the data. Make a drawing.
See Figure 2–16 .

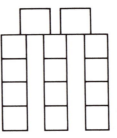

Figure 2–16

Note that the first arch required 9 blocks, the second arch required 5 more, or a total of 14 blocks. The exploration reveals one way we can resolve the problem. We could continue drawing the arches until we have all 12.

3. Select a strategy.
Make a table, Reduce and expand. Look for a pattern.
Let's begin with 1 arch. The drawing in Figure 2-16 showed us that we would need 9 blocks. When we added a second arch, we now needed 14 blocks. Let's add a third arch (see Figure 2-17). We need 19 blocks.

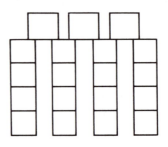

Figure 2–17

Lets record the data in a table.

Number of Arches	1	2	3	. . .
Number of Blocks	9	14	19	. . .

There seems to be a pattern. After the first arch, which required 9 blocks, each additional arch requires 5 more blocks. We could now continue the table until we reach 12 arches.

4. Find the answer.
Carry through your strategy. Estimate the answer.
If 3 arches required 19 blocks, and 12 is 4 × 3, then 12 arches should require approximately 4 × 19 or 76 blocks. To obtain the answer, we will continue the table until we reach 12 arches.

Number of Arches	1	2	3	4	5	6	7	8	9	10	11	12
Number of Blocks	9	14	19	24	29	34	39	44	49	54	59	64

Lorenzo needed 64 blocks to make all 12 arches.

5. Reflect and extend.
Compare your answer to your estimate. Did you answer the question? Verify your answer. Look for variations. Ask "What if" questions. Describe the solution.
Our estimate was 76; our actual answer was 64. The answer is "in the ballpark." We solved the problem by making a drawing and a table. The answer was obtained by extending the table until we reached 12 arches. We simulated the action with pencil and paper.
Let's extend the problem to a mathematical formula. Find the pattern rule. The number of blocks required is 5 times the number of arches plus 4, or $5a + 4$ (where a = the number of arches).
What if there were 30 arches? How many blocks would we need? What if each column required 5 blocks?
What if each arch required 3 blocks on top of 2 columns?

PROBLEM   Mrs. Arnez bought 45 calculators for the mathematics laboratory. *The Mathematician* calculators cost $25 each, and the *Arithmetician* calculators cost $4 each. If she spent $600, how many of each type did she buy?

Discussion   *1. Read and think.*
Describe the setting and visualize the action. What is being asked? What information is given?

The problem says that 45 calculators were bought. There were two kinds of calculators. Some cost $25 each, the rest cost $4 each. The total cost was $600. We are asked to find how many of each type were bought.

2. Explore and plan.
Organize the data. Represent the data in a table.
The first thought is that the sum of the two numbers we are looking for must equal 45. When we multiply each of these numbers by the appropriate cost and total the results, we must get a total of $600.

3. Select a strategy.
Guess and test. Keep track of each guess and its results in the table.

4. Find the answer.
Carry out your strategy.

Mathematician		Arithmetician			
Number	Cost	Number	Cost	Total Cost	
40	$1,000	5	$20	$1,020	Too Large!
30	$ 750	15	$60	$ 810	Too Large!
20	$ 500	25	$100	$ 600	Correct!

There are 45 calculators and their total cost is $600. She bought 20 *Mathematicians* and 25 *Arithmeticians*.

5. Reflect and extend.
Did you answer the question? Verify your answer. Look for variations. Ask "What if" questions. Describe the solutions.
We solved the problem by guess and test and recorded the results in a table. We refined each guess based on the results of the previous one(s). Could there be other sets of guesses? Could she have bought 24 of the *Mathematician* calculators? Why or why not?
Could she have bought 150 of the *Arithmetician* calculators? Why or Why not?
When Mrs. Arnez went to pick up the calculators and pay the bill, she was told of the new October Bonus Deal; for every 2 *Mathematicians* she had bought, they would give her 1 free *Arithmetician*. How many calculators did she take away?

It should be apparent as one proceeds through the problem-solving heuristics in the last two model problems that reasoning, critical thinking, and creative thinking, all occur throughout virtually every step. It is our contention that, when properly presented, the use of problem-solving heuristics will result in the practice necessary to develop good reasoning powers. Thus, problems will provide the vehicle by which we will teach both problem solving and reasoning.

It is obvious that the actions described in the two sets of heuristics given in this chapter are virtually the same. The reasoning heuristics and the problem-solving heuristics differ only in vocabulary.

CHAPTER THREE

The Teaching
of Reasoning
and Problem Solving

CHARACTERISTICS OF A GOOD REASONER AND PROBLEM SOLVER

Good problem solvers and reasoners exhibit similar traits. Although we cannot state precisely what it is that makes them excel, there are certain common characteristics exhibited by those who perform well on such tasks. For example, they have a *desire* to solve problems. Problems interest them and offer a challenge. Their curiosity is easily aroused, and they enjoy pursuing the solution to a logical conclusion. They are naturally *inquisitive*, their thoughts go beyond the obvious to the "why" of the answer. Much like mountain climbers, problem solvers like to solve problems because the problems are there.

Problem solvers and reasoners are extremely *persevering* when solving problems. In many situations, their initial attempts do not lead to success. This is to be expected, or they wouldn't be solving a problem—merely working on an exercise. They are not easily discouraged. They go back and try new approaches again and again. They have a large repertoire of things to try. They persist with the problem despite opposition or discouragement to their ideas. They are reluctant to give up on a problem. They refuse to quit!

These people exhibit unbridled *curiosity*. They are eager to investigate new situations, they are inquisitive, and even when an answer has been obtained, they go on. Their thinking is *divergent*. It goes beyond seeking a specific response to a specific question. They do not limit themselves to the obvious. They will ask themselves many "What if?" questions, changing conditions within the problem and determining what effect these changes have on their initial answer.

Good reasoners and problem solvers are not afraid to *speculate*, to *conjecture*, or to *guess*! They are risk-takers, not afraid of being wrong or unsuccessful when they try to solve a problem. They will make educated guesses at answers, and then attempt to verify these guesses. They know how to refine their guesses on the basis of what previous guesses showed them, until they find a satisfactory answer.

Good problem solvers and reasoners show an ability to skip some of the steps in the solution process. They make connections quickly, notice irrelevant detail, and often require only a few examples to generalize. They may show a lack of concern about neatness while developing their solution process.

We suggest that good reasoners and problem solvers are students who hold conversations with themselves. They know what questions to ask themselves, and what to do with the answers they receive as they think through the problem.

Above all, good reasoners and problem solvers are people who can focus on the task at hand. Although they might be tempted to move tangentially, they know the direction they must take to satisfy the requirements of the given situation.

THE CLASSROOM OF THE '90S AND BEYOND

Reasoning and problem solving are process skills. They are quite different from performance skills such as addition, subtraction, multiplication, and division. The teaching of process skills dictates a change in the classroom environment. By classroom environment we include the physical makeup of the classroom, the roles of teacher and the students, and their interaction. The traditional classroom with its rows of seats, with children attentively and passively watching as the teacher performs in front of the room (a teacher-centered classroom), is not conducive to the development of a thinking individual.

The new classroom must include movable furniture to permit small-group activity, learning stations, technology centers, and a resource center with manipulatives and library materials. In this environment, the teacher choreographs activities and experiences that involve interaction and foster communication between students and teachers, between students and students. The teacher asks thought-provoking questions that force students to reflect and respond with statements, thoughts, and questions of their own.

Most classroom teachers have had little experience with the role they are being asked to play. Thus, we cannot expect teachers to move easily into this new situation without in-service instructional programs. In the past, the teacher's role was mainly limited to imparting knowledge. In this new environment, the teacher must learn how to initiate and to utilize student responses that open or extend their reasoning skills. This chapter will be devoted to specific suggestions for creating and operating in this new and different classroom environment.

1. Create a non-threatening environment.

Fundamental to this new classroom is an atmosphere in which the student feels free, and indeed is encouraged, to put forth suggestions and make conjectures without fear of negative criticism or ridicule. In the beginning, children who are unaccustomed to expressing themselves freely may make extraneous or irrelevant comments just to test how far they can go. This is to be expected and will gradually diminish as the students realize that they have the freedom to be part of the discussion, with no recriminations. However, a word of caution is needed here. You, as the teacher, must be prepared for answers that, on the surface, appear to be "flip" or "wise" in their delivery. You must carefully examine and consider each. In many cases, these may have a great deal of merit, and be the result of sound creative thinking. Even "way out" responses can be used to initiate a discussion to the advantage of everyone.

PROBLEM Supply the next two terms in the sequence 2, 4, 6.

Discussion This problem was initially presented in Chapter One, with several possible answers given. However, some highly unusual answers (to say the least) have also been given by students. For example:

(a) 2, 4, 6, <u>84</u>, <u>112</u>
(b) 2, 4, 6, <u>6</u>,   <u>6</u>
(c) 2, 4, 6, <u>$1</u>

Do these make sense? How should a teacher respond to each in a non-threatening manner? In the first two illustrations, the teacher's response might be to ask the student to give 1 more term, and ask the entire class, "Does anyone recognize the pattern rule? " In (a), the respondent said, "They're all even and getting bigger!" In (b), the response was "I got tired and just wrote sixes!" In (c), the entire class began to laugh and, in unison, joined in, "Two bits, four bits, six bits, a dollar," a well-known cheer at sporting events. In this non-threatening environment, the teacher welcomes these responses because they provide an opportunity for the children to engage in creative thought and to express themselves verbally, thus enhancing their communication skills. Here are some suggestions for dealing with student responses:

Instead of Saying	Say
"You're right!"	"What led you to that conclusion?"
"You're wrong!"	"How did you get that?"
"Here's how to do it!"	"What might we try?"
	"What do you think would happen if . . .?"

One of our major goals as we seek to create better problem solvers and reasoners is to develop a critical and investigative attitude in our students. This goal can best be achieved by using phrases similar to those above, instead of merely terminating the thought process with a simple "yes" or "no." The interaction fostered by the alternative statements helps students achieve the goals and meet these expectations.

2. Have your students work together in a variety of groupings.

Small-group activities, sometimes referred to as cooperative or collaborative learning, have been shown to yield excellent results in fostering communication and thinking skills. The interaction between students helps them learn to modify one another's thinking and to clarify their own. They will also learn to express their thoughts more clearly by the use of precise language, especially mathematical terminology. Students will find it difficult to communicate with each other unless they use language that the group can agree on.

Be certain that, within the groups, each student has an assigned task, and that this task rotates. Thus, each student should have the experience of being a recorder within the group and a reporter to the class at large. Problems should be assigned to the class as a whole, and each group should pursue the solution. At an appropriate time, the group reporter discusses his or her group's solution with the class, and the class then interacts with each group.

What does the teacher do while this action is taking place? Primarily the teacher serves as a consultant. He or she moves from group to group, participating in each group's discussion. Be careful not to dominate the discussion, but make suggestions when appropriate. Remember that the goal of this model of instruction is to foster discussion and creative and critical thinking.

This small-group model is similar to and an outgrowth of the think-tank or brainstorming process in industry. Rarely does one person solve a major problem alone. Although the final decision does fall on one person, group participation, deliberation, and input are integral parts of the problem-solving process, which ultimately leads to decision making. A student's inability to participate in a group process could conceivably eliminate him or her from a future occupation.

The groundwork for cooperative learning in small groups should be laid in the elementary school grades. The classroom teacher must provide guidance and practice in the particular skills involved in sharing ideas. The teacher should encourage *all* students to contribute to the discussion. Keep in mind that in this form of instruction:

1. There should be no verbal evaluation of any kind by the teacher.
2. There should be critical analysis of all suggestions by members of the group, but no negative nor derogatory comments.
3. Everyone is encouraged to allow his or her imagination to run rampant.
4. Students are encouraged to put forth as many ideas as possible.
5. Everyone is encouraged to build on or modify the ideas of others.

The important task is to work together toward solving the problem.

For the teacher of mathematics, this form of learning is particularly effective for developing problem-solving and reasoning skills. The focus of the groups is on resolving the problem situation, and it is important that each group have the opportunity to present its solution(s). Each group discusses its solution and defends it against critical examination by the other groups, thus forcing the team into an analysis of its own thinking, referred to as the metacognitive process. This will be discussed at a later point.

ACTIVITY   Divide your class into groups of 4 or 5 students. Each group should be provided with a pair of totally unrelated words such as:

(a) telephone—umbrella
(b) baseball—ocean
(c) pen—pizza
(d) elephant—lollipop
(e) hot dogs—hat
(f) sunglasses—flashlight

Notice that the words in each pair do not appear to have anything in common. It is the group's task to connect the two words in a problem. Be creative and use your imagination.

ACTIVITY   "Notice" is a quiz that is administered to students in groups. The entire group must determine whether each statement is true or false. Here are some sample statements you might use:

(a) The Statue of Liberty uses her right hand to hold the torch. (True)
(b) A record on a turntable will turn clockwise. (True)
(c) Page 82 of a book is a right-hand page. (False)
(d) Most pencils have 8 sides. (False)
(e) Q is the only letter that is missing on a telephone dial or pushbutton pad. (False)

ACTIVITY   Students are divided into groups of 5 or 6. Each group is given the task of building the highest possible tower out of the available materials in a fixed time period. The group must decide who will be responsible for the various tasks required to build the tower. Materials might consist of the following: small boxes (single-serving cereal boxes, for example), construction paper, adhesive tape, rolls from inside paper towels, pieces of styrofoam, metal scraps, pipe cleaners, etc. The only restriction is that the tower may not be attached in any way to the walls or ceiling for support.

Problems in which students have to list all the possible outcomes lend themselves well to the group discussion method. The group will decide when all possible outcomes have been listed.

PROBLEM   Your group has been given $1,000 to spend in a 24-hour period. How would you spend the money? You may buy only one of each item your group selects.

PROBLEM   Anthony was in the restroom at 3:00. When he came out, he discovered that his school bus had already left. It was raining hard. How can he get home?

We do not advocate that students spend all their class time working in small groups, but the group process is a good method for allowing students to develop respect for one another's abilities and to learn to look for many possibilities in solving problems. It also permits the children to share and refine ideas. Small groups are most effective when discovery is involved. However, for performance skills, a more traditional classroom approach may be necessary.

3. Raise creative, constructive, thought-provoking questions.

Teachers should keep in mind that in dealing with the development of process skills, we should not take the students directly to the answer by showing them a solution. Instead, ask questions that will provide the students with guidance and direction and allow for a wide range of responses. Give them time to think before they respond to your questions. Research indicates that the average teacher allows less than three seconds for students to respond to a question. Problem solving and reasoning are complex processes. You must allow time for reflection. Don't rush your questions.

In trying to guide your students through the reasoning experience, use open-ended questions frequently. Questions such as, "Count the number of . . . ,"Find all . . . ,"How many . . . ," "What conclusions can you draw?," "What questions can you answer?" or "What would you do?" are non-threatening questions that can lead to successful student responses. In addition, as we have stated before, the use of "What if" questions is a viable way of extending the child's critical and creative thinking processes.

PROBLEM   How many squares can you find in Figure 3–1?

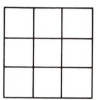

Figure 3–1

Discussion Note the question being asked! It deviates from the tradition by asking "How many can *you* find?" as opposed to "How many are there?" Since the question asks for how many squares *you* can find, it cannot be answered incorrectly even if the student can only find a few squares. You should lead the students to see all the squares of various sizes, but students are not really wrong if they see only 9.

Throughout the reasoning process, let your questions cause the students to reflect on how they are attacking the problems. Have them explain their approach, and, if possible, why they took that route. Examine their responses carefully; ask questions about key points. Ask many "What if" questions. Ask students, "What new problems does this suggest?" or "How else might I ask this question?"

Other questions might include:

1. Do you recognize any patterns?
2. What is another way to approach this problem?
3. What kind of problem that you've seen before does this problem remind you of?
4. What would happen if
   • the conditions of the problem were changed to . . . ?
   • we imposed additional conditions?
5. What further exploration of this problem can you suggest?
6. What additional questions might you answer?

PROBLEM Amy uses 15 chips for a contest. She wrote the numeral 1 on the first chip. The second chip has the numeral 5 on it, and the third chip has a numeral 9. If Amy continues in this way, what numeral will be on the last chip?

Discussion We can write the numerals in the following array:

1	5	9	13	17
21	25	29	33	37
41	45	49	53	57

You might now ask some of the following questions to stimulate class discussion:

(a) Do you recognize a pattern? What is it?
(b) What if Amy had only 5 chips?
(c) Can you draw a picture of all 15 chips?
(d) What numeral would be on the fifth chip?

When asking questions of students, be careful that:

1. You do not change or alter the question while the students are considering it.
2. You give the students ample time before repeating the question or modifying it.
3. You do not answer your own question, even when you are certain that the students have finished their responses. Perhaps then an additional hint or comment might lead them in the right direction.

4. Encourage creativity of thought and imagination.

In a non-threatening classroom atmosphere, students should be as free-thinking as they wish. You should not penalize "way out" answers if they show some thought by the students. Again, keep in mind that one of our major goals is to develop creative thinking. This can only be done in an environment in which the child feels free to take a risk with no fear of recrimination.

ACTIVITY   Write a story using the information shown in Figure 3–2.

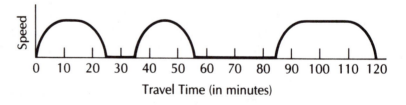

Travel Time (in minutes)

Figure 3–2

Discussion   The above graph showing travel time and speed can lead to several scenarios. One might be that of a family out for a drive. The first pause shows a stop of about 10 minutes, which might be for gas; the more extended stop might be for lunch. Have the students write stories interpreting the data shown and share their stories with the class.

PROBLEM   In the near future, there may be a new state added to the United States. How would you design the field of stars on the American flag to include 51 stars?

PROBLEM   On Glenda's new clock, both hands are the same size. When she looked at her clock just now, she noticed that one hand was on the 12 and one was on the 4. How could she tell what time it was?

PROBLEM   In the election for class president, Marian and Liu each received 13 votes; Marcus received 6. How can the tie be broken?

The four activities suggested above will often yield responses that are quite different from what was anticipated. Students may interpret what is given and what is asked for in several ways. Each interpretation may be different in meaning, yet quite appropriate in thought. In all cases, you must lead the class in a critical discussion of what led to these various interpretations.

Systematic trial and error and careful, selective guessing are both creative techniques to use. (How often have teachers been heard to say to a student, "Do you *know* or are you just guessing?") Guessing, or careful trial-and-error reasoning, should be practiced and encouraged. It is important to be a good guesser.

PROBLEM   Helen has $1.05 in coins with no pennies. What coins does she have?

Discussion   This problem has 43 different answers. Encourage the students to find as many as they can, keep track of them, and share their findings. Hands-on manipulatives can be used to solve this problem, with a table to keep track of the guesses and results.

We can ask a variety of questions to inspire students to think and reason. For example,

(a) What is the maximum number of coins possible?
(21—all nickels)
(b) What is the minimum number of coins possible?
(2—a silver dollar and a nickel).
(c) What if Helen had no nickels?
(2 possibilities—1 quarter and 8 dimes, or 3 quarters and 3 dimes.)

Notice that if you change the conditions of the problem (i.e., What if there were no nickels?), the number of answers is limited to 2.

PROBLEM   Roscoe, Tony, and Miriam ordered a large hoagie sandwich and had cut it cut into 3 equal parts. Just before they began to eat, Alice joined them. How should they divide the sandwich so that they will each have the same amount?

Discussion   One way of solving this problem is to assign chip values to each of the 3 original parts of the hoagie. Each original piece might be worth a green chip. Now trade each of the green chips for 4 red chips. If Roscoe, Tony, and Miriam each give 1 red chip to Alice, everyone will now have 3 red chips. Interpret these actions in terms of thirds and fourths of the original sandwich. What part of the original hoagie did each person give to Alice? What part of the original hoagie does each person have now? What fractional part of the sandwich is represented by each color chip?

PROBLEM   Miguel and his grandfather are comparing their ages. Interestingly enough, their ages have the same digits, only reversed. The difference between their ages is 54 years and the sum of the digits in each age is 10. How old is each of them?

Discussion   Students in the upper grades might complete this problem by solving a pair of linear equations with two unknowns simultaneously, but creative use of guess and test can make this problem suitable for a problem-solving activity at the lower grade levels as well. You should guide students towards the following solution:

1. First, list all the 2-digit numbers whose digit-sum is 10:

   19,   28,   37,   46,   55,   64,   73,   82,   91

   You should pause at this point, and let the students consider what to do next. Hopefully, this will lead to someone suggesting that the class subtract.
2. Next, subtract those pairs of numbers which have the same digits:

$$91 - 19 = 72$$
$$82 - 28 = 54$$
$$73 - 37 = 36$$
$$64 - 46 = 18$$

At this point, you might consider asking the students how they know that 82 and 28 are the *only* pair of 2-digit ages that satisfy the original problem. What happened to the age of 55? Why wasn't it used?

5. Create an atmosphere of success.

The old adage "Nothing succeeds like success" holds true in the mathematics classroom. If students are successful in the introductory problems they encounter, they will be more willing to attempt more difficult problems. Choose the problems you use carefully. Begin with relatively simple problems, to ensure a reasonable degree of success. If students are successful, they are likely to be "turned on" to problem solving, whereas repeated failure or constant frustration can have a devastating effect on motivation, attitude, and the desire to continue. However, remember that success must truly be earned, not just given.

The breadth and depth of knowledge required, as well as the sequence of problems chosen, should be kept in mind as major criteria for developing problem-solving situations. Present a problem to the class and delete the question given. Have the students decide what questions they could answer from the data provided. In a situation such as this, every student can achieve some degree of success. You can be certain that the original question will appear as one of the children's suggestions.

PROBLEM Alex and Helen went to the local supermarket. They bought 3 pounds of bananas at 45¢ a pound, 2 loaves of bread at $1.25 a loaf, and 3 boxes of cereal for $10.00. They gave the clerk a $20 bill. (How much change did they receive?)

Discussion This traditional type of problem can be used to assure success for everyone in the class if the teacher modifies it. Instead of attempting to get the final answer, ask the children what questions they *can* answer or what conclusions they can reach from the given material. This requires a careful analysis by the children (one of our reasoning goals), and also promotes conjecturing (to be discussed later). This type of discussion helps develop the child's ability to analyze a problem. Individual questions that might be answered include:

(a) What is the price of each item?
(b) What is the amount spent on bananas?
(c) What is the cost of the cereal?
(d) What is the price of 1 box of cereal? (Can you tell? Why or why not?)
(e) How much did they spend altogether?

(f) How much change did they receive? (Of course.)

Success in problem solving means more than obtaining the correct answer. When the students become absorbed in a problem and make a sustained attempt at solution, they should be made to realize that this is also success.

6. Encourage your students to solve problems.

For our students to become good problem solvers and reasoners, they must be constantly exposed to and involved in each of these activities. If a student refuses even to attempt to solve a problem, there can be no problem-solving activity taking place. In learning to ride a bicycle, for example, the "theory" can go just so far; eventually, the real ability to ride must come from actual riding! Problem solving is the same. Students must solve problems! Students must use their reasoning skills. The teacher should try to find situations that are of interest to students. Listen to them as they talk among themselves; they will often tell you about the things that interest them. (Problems derived from television, food, sports, and science fiction usually generate enthusiasm among students.) In many cases, group activities will encourage students to participate who might otherwise be reluctant to become involved.

PROBLEM   While in space, an astronaut exercises 20 minutes each day. How many minutes will she exercise in 1 week?

Discussion   The problem should interest children, since astronauts and space travel have a natural appeal. The problem requires that the children draw on the fact that there are 7 days in a week. They may also wish to convert 140 minutes into hours and minutes.

PROBLEM   In the circus, there are 9 elephants. Each elephant eats 5 tons of hay in a month. How much hay will all the elephants eat in a year?

Discussion   This problem is similar to many basic textbook problems. Yet the setting of a circus, with elephants, is much more appealing to students and creates a greater desire among them to solve the problem.

ACTIVITY   Take several exercises from the students' textbook. Encourage the students to change the setting of each problem to one that is more interesting to them. Emphasize that their problems must contain the same data as the original's.

Discussion   One effect of this activity will be to force the students to understand what the problem is really about. At the same time, they will be engaged in creating problems similar to the original but more interesting to them.

ACTIVITY   Present your students with a series of still pictures that can be sequenced. Perhaps you might take a comic strip from the local newspaper, mount it on oaktag, and then cut the frames apart. Have your students arrange the pictures in a logical order and then explain the reason for their choice. This activity promotes good analysis and improves reasoning skills. Comic strips are fun for children and encourage them to participate in the activity.

ACTIVITY   Present students with problems that do not contain specific numbers. Ask them to supply reasonable numerical data and then tell how they might solve each problem. Focus the students' attention on the larger issue of a general strategy as well as on the specific details of the particular problem at hand. If difficulties arise, make yourself available to *help* students; *do not* solve the problems for them.
Example: Arlene bought a container of milk, an orange, and a tunafish sandwich for lunch. How can she be certain that she has enough money?
Example: Three skydivers jumped out of an airplane that was flying high above the ground. After free-falling for awhile, their parachutes snapped open and they dropped gently to the ground, holding hands all the way. How long did it take them to reach the ground?
Example: Matt's computer program has more lines than Bernie's. Joe's program has more lines than Matt's. How many lines are in Matt's program?

Unfortunately, in some classrooms, teachers give the impression that there is only one way to solve each problem. Thus, creative solutions are sometimes discouraged. If we are to encourage our students to solve problems, we should open the discussion to a variety of solutions whenever possible. Try to solve problems in more than one way. Teachers should not only accept, but should encourage and discuss alternate approaches. In fact, small groups should be formed, and each group assigned the task of discovering different solutions. These must also be discussed. Problem solving becomes a regular, ongoing activity, rather than an occasional lesson. Thus, the apprehension that children have towards word problems will be eliminated.

PROBLEM Three members of the Mendoza family have their birthdays on 3 consecutive days in June. The sum of the 3 dates is 42. What are the dates of their birthdays?

Discussion One solution to the problem might be to guess and test. Someone might guess 10, 11, and 12. Their sum is 33, which is too small. The next guess might be 20, 21, and 22. This sum is 63, which is too large. The students continue refining successive guesses until they reach the answer. Another way to solve the problem is to use elementary algebra. Let x, $x + 1$, and $x + 2$ represent the three dates. Then

$$(x) + (x + 1) + (x + 2) = 42$$

Another approach is to divide 42 by 3, obtaining 14. Then choose one number on either side of 14, yielding 13, 14, and 15 as the 3 consecutive dates in June. (Notice that this is equivalent to the algebraic equation $(x - 1) + (x) + (x + 1) = 42$.)

7. Help your students to become critical readers.

Reading is fundamental to the development of problem-solving and reasoning skills. Most problem situations that children encounter, particularly in school, are presented in written format. Reading in mathematics is quite different from reading in general. Reading mathematics material requires more careful analysis and attention to detail. *Critical thinking is paramount.* Students cannot merely skim through a verbal problem. As part of "reading" we include the ability to extract information that may appear in pictures, requiring critical observational skills. Through problem solving, we can achieve all of these objectives.

Problems have a basic anatomy. This anatomy of a problem consists of four parts: a setting, facts, a question, and distractors. All problems need not contain all of these—the setting and/or the distractors are not always present.

Fundamental to solving a problem is understanding the setting of the problem. If the setting is unfamiliar to students, it will be impossible for them to solve the problem. Some time should be devoted to having the students relate what is taking place in a problem. This not only gives the students practice in reading for understanding, but helps them develop their communication skills, so vital to the reasoning process.

PROBLEM   There are 8 students entered in the fifth grade checkers tournament. In each game, 2 of the students play against each other. The loser of each game is eliminated from the tournament. How many games are needed to find a champion?

Discussion   Although this problem seems simple to an adult, it is not necessarily simple to youngsters. Ask the children to describe in their own words what is going on in the problem. Questions may be asked to help extract this information. For example,

(a) How many people are involved?
(b) What are they doing?
(c) Where is the action taking place?
(d) How is a person eliminated from the tournament?
(e) How many people must be eliminated?

Many activities should be used to help students sharpen their ability to read critically and carefully for meaning. One such technique is to have students underline or circle words that they consider to be critical facts in a problem. Discuss these words with the class. Have the students indicate why they consider these particular words to be critical.

PROBLEM   Mrs. Flynn's children were picking fruit in the orchard. When they came back, they had 45 apples and peaches together. Upon counting, Mrs. Flynn discovered that there were peaches for every apple. How many apples were there?

Discussion   Mrs. Flynn's children were picking fruit in the orchard. When they came back, they had <u>45 apples and peaches</u> altogether. Upon counting, Mrs. Flynn discovered that there were <u>2 peaches for every apple. How many apples were there?</u>

ACTIVITY   Write a problem on a slip of paper. Have a student read the problem silently, put the slip of paper away, and then relate the problem in his or her own words to the rest of the class. In this way, students often reveal whether they have found the facts that are really important to the solution of the problem, or whether they have missed the point entirely.

ACTIVITY   Show a problem on a transparency with the overhead projector. After a short period of time, turn the projector off and have the class restate the problem in their own words.

ACTIVITY   Have one student be the "problem maker." Ask 3 different children to supply 1 fact each (these may be totally unrelated) The problem maker must then write a word problem using the facts she or he has been given. Have the class solve the problem.

ACTIVITY   One way to encourage practice in reading mathematics problems slowly and for understanding is to mimeograph a page from a mathematics textbook, cut the page into pieces like those of a jigsaw puzzle, and have the students put the page together again.

Many words have a special meaning in mathematics that is different from the everyday meaning. The class should discuss a list of such words, with their various meanings. A beneficial project is to have the students compile a "dictionary" in which each word is defined in both mathematical and in other contexts.

ACTIVITY   Discuss the different meanings of the following words:

times	volume	prime	power
difference	foot	order	even
pound	face	figure	odd
count	chord	root	

After your students have gained an understanding of a problem and can relate it in their own words, they should also be able to identify the question to be answered.

ACTIVITY   Give students a set of problems and have them underline or circle the sentence that tells them what they must find. Note that this "question" may be given in the interrogative form or may be stated in the declarative form.

Example: There are 3 boys and 2 girls watching the circus clowns perform. <u>How many children are watching the clowns?</u>

Example: Michael has just planted a new garden. He wants to put a rope around it to keep people from walking on it. <u>Find the amount of rope he will need</u> if the garden is in the shape of a rectangle that is 16 feet long and 8 feet wide.

ACTIVITY

Every problem must have a question in order to be considered a problem. *What's your question?* is an activity that requires the students to supply a reasonable question based on a given situation. Asking students to do this forces them to analyze the situation, identify the facts, and work out the relationships between the 2. This is a needed skill for problem solving and reasoning.

Example: Ralph is 16 years old, Marcia is 19 years old, and Lynn is 15 years old.

Make this a problem by supplying an appropriate question.

Example: Sally and Luisa went shopping in the mall. Sally had brought $30 to spend. She bought a blouse for $12.95 and a record for $9.50.

Make this a problem by supplying an appropriate question.

The information necessary to solve a problem sometimes appears in verbal form. At other times it may appear in picture form. Give the students activities similar to the ones that follow to help them determine which facts in a problem are important.

ACTIVITY

Read the following paragraph. Then answer the questions.

Mr. and Mrs. Salvatore and their 3 children went to the Aquarium of the Oceans. Tickets cost $8 for adults and $4 for children. The porpoise show ran from 1:00 P.M. to 1:45 P.M. The fish in the big pool were fed from 2:00 P.M. to 2:30 P.M. They stayed in the aquarium for exactly 6 hours, and left at 4:00 P.M.

1. What is the name of the aquarium?
2. How much do adult tickets cost?
3. How much do children's tickets cost?
4. How long is the porpoise show?
5. At what time do they begin feeding the fish in the big pool?
6. At what time do they finish feeding the fish in the big pool?

7. When did the Salvatores leave the aquarium?
8. When did they enter the aquarium?
9. How many members of the Salvatore family went to the aquarium?
10. How much did it cost for tickets to the aquarium?

ACTIVITY   Look at the toys in Figure 3–3. Then answer the questions.

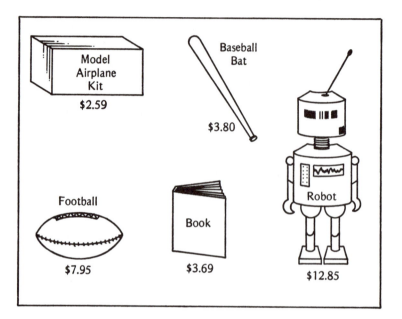

Figure 3–3

1. Which toy costs $2.59 ?
2. How much does the football cost?
3. Which toy is the most expensive?
4. Which toy is the least expensive?
5. Which toys cost less than $5.00 ?
6. Which toys cost more than $6.00 ?
7. Miriam has $10 to spend. Which toys can she buy?

Most of the questions in these two activities can be answered directly from the statements in the text or the facts in the drawing. However, some of the questions may require either some computation or use of inference. To many of us who are more experienced than our students, these inferences may be apparent. It is most important that the students learn to differentiate between what is given directly and what can be extrapolated from the given information.

ACTIVITY   Read the paragraph and answer each of the questions that follow it. Then tell whether the answer was obtained by direct observation or by a calculation or an inference.

Last Sunday, Eloise and her two older brothers Jamie and Matt, went on a fishing trip. Their mother packed them each two sandwiches. Three of the sandwiches were roast beef and these were made on rye bread. The other three were tunafish and they were on whole wheat bread.

They left their house at 5:00 A.M. and two hours later they began fishing in the Lake. After about one hour of fishing, Matt, the oldest brother, said, "I'm hungry! I'm going to eat!" and so he ate a tunafish sandwich. Eloise and Jamie decided to join him, and they each ate a roast beef sandwich. About 11:00 o'clock, each of them ate another sandwich, but this time they each ate a sandwich that was different from the one that each had eaten previously. After seven hours at the lake they went home with their catch of 18 fish. Their mother asked who had caught the fish. Matt said, "I caught half of them and Eloise caught three more than Jamie."

1. How many sandwiches did their mother pack?
2. How many tunafish sandwiches did each of them eat?
3. How many fish did they catch?
4. What time did they leave their house?
5. On what day did they go fishing?
6. What time did they start fishing?
7. What time did they leave for home?
8. At what time did Matt eat a tunafish sandwich?
9. At what time did the youngest person eat a tunafish sandwich?
10. How long did they fish?
11. By noon, they had caught 10 fish. How many fish did they catch in the afternoon?
12. Who is the middle child in age?
13. How many fish did each person catch?

Reading a problem also means being able to discriminate between necessary and unnecessary information. In many cases, information is put into a problem merely to serve as a distractor. In other cases, necessary data may have been omitted. We strongly recommend that students be given activities that will enable them to distinguish between necessary and superfluous data, as well as to determine when there is insufficient data to solve the problem. Students must not only determine that facts are missing, but should also be required to supply the facts that are needed, and these facts must be reasonable. The problem should then be solved by using the student-supplied facts. Time should be spent examining the relationships between different facts supplied and the different answers that result.

ACTIVITY   Give the students a problem in written form. Include extra information. Tell the students to cross out what they think is unnecessary. Have them read what remains. Can they now solve the problem?
Example: On the second Saturday in July, 2 patrols of Girl Scouts went berrypicking. There were 9 girls in each patrol. One patrol picked 18 cans and the other patrol picked 12 cans. How many cans of berries were picked altogether?

Discussion   Students should cross out the number of scouts in each patrol, 9. "On the second Saturday in July" is also a distractor and should be eliminated.
Example: Mr. Chen's station wagon gets only 12 miles per gallon of gas. Gasoline costs $1.19 a gallon. When he returned home from his trip to the national park, he filled up his tank with 15 gallons of gasoline. How much did he spend for gasoline?

Discussion   Students should recognize that the miles per gallon and the destination are excess information.

ACTIVITY   Give the students a problem in written form. Omit one piece of necessary information. Have one student identify what is missing. Then have a second student supply a *reasonable* fact so that the problem can be solved. Now have the class solve the problem.
Example: The temperature dropped 2° each hour that Stan was at the beach. He stayed at the beach for 5 hours. What was the temperature when Stan left the beach?

Discussion   The students should recognize that the answer depends upon the temperature at the start of Stan's stay at the beach. Be certain that the temperature the students supply is a reasonable one for beach weather.
Example: Lucy gets to keep 6¢ for each newspaper she delivers on her paper route. How much did she earn last Saturday?

Discussion   Be certain that the students supply a reasonable number of papers for a person to deliver on a paper route.

ACTIVITY   Prepare a collection of problems on 3"× 5" cards. Some of the problems should have excess information; others should have missing data. Students must decide which is which, and supply the data needed to solve the problem if facts are missing. Then divide the class into groups. Have each group prepare similar problems with missing and/or excess information. Have the groups exchange cards and solve each other's problems.

Critical reading includes the ability to decide when the information included in a problem is contradictory or inconsistent. Students should be given problems in which there are contradictory and inconsistent statements. These should be read and discussed by the group to determine where the inconsistencies lie.

ACTIVITY

Give students sets of sentence pairs similar to the following sets. Have them determine whether the sentences in each set can be true at the same time. If not, tell why not.

1. (a) John took his twin sisters, Amy and Ann, to the movies.
   (b) The ages of the three children are 17, 12, and 10.
2. (a) Susan is younger than Greg.
   (b) Susan's birthday is in April and Greg's birthday is in October. (Greg could have been born a year or more before Susan.)
3. (a) Anita is 5 years older than Peg.
   (b) Two years ago, Anita was 3 years older than Peg. (Anita will always be 5 years older than Peg.)
4. (a) One dog can jump over a 3-foot wide stream.
   (b) Five dogs can jump over a 15-foot stream.
5. (a) Tomorrow is Tuesday.
   (b) Yesterday was Monday.

ACTIVITY

Have students read the following paragraphs. Determine the errors.

1. Mr. and Mrs. Gomez took their 3 children, Anthony, Dolores, and Francine, to the baseball game between the Dodgers and the Giants. The game started at 8:00 P.M. General admission tickets were $5 each. The game lasted 3 hours, with the final score Dodgers 5, Giants 3. They left as soon as the game ended, and arrived home at 10:30 P.M. When they were in their house, Mr. Gomez remarked, " What a wonderful time we had, and it only cost us $10!"
2. Mrs. Cardone took her 24 fourth graders on a picnic. She packed 40 sandwiches, so that each child could have 2 sandwiches to eat. They arrived at the picnic grounds at exactly 10:00 A.M. Immediately, 18 children went to play baseball, 12 went to play volleyball, and the remaining 6 helped Mrs. Cardone unpack the lunch. They all left for home after exactly 6 hours at the picnic grounds, and ar-

rived back at their school at exactly 2:30 P.M., just in time to be picked up by their parents.

ACTIVITY Problem Reader—Problem Solver is an activity that helps to sharpen students' ability to read and comprehend a problem quickly and accurately. It is particularly effective in helping students to ascertain the important elements of a problem. The students in the class are divided into teams of 4. One pair of students on each team is designated the problem readers, and while the other pair is designated the problem solvers. The problem solvers close their eyes while a problem is displayed by the overhead projector for about 30 seconds. (The time will depend on the ability of the students and the difficulty level of the problem itself.) During the time the problem is displayed, the problem readers may take any notes or make any drawings that they think necessary. The problem is then taken off the overhead, and the problem readers present the problem (as they saw it) to their partners, who must solve it. The problem readers and the problem solvers then reverse roles and play the game again.

ACTIVITY Divide the class into 3 or 4 teams consisting of 5 to 8 students on each team. Tell the students that they are going on a problem scavenger hunt. Each team must find problems in their textbooks as asked for on the list of items they will receive. Present each team with the same list of items, similar to the following:

1. Find a problem that has a setting in a supermarket.
2. Find a problem that deals with sports.
3. Find a problem where the answer is an amount of money.
4. Find a problem where some of the information is given in a picture.
5. Find a problem where the answer is in hours.
6. Find a problem that contains too much information.
7. Find a problem that contains insufficient information.
8. Find a problem where subtraction is used to find the answer.

Activities such as these can all be used to help our students become better and more critical readers. There is a strong link between language and how well the students understand the ideas and concepts under discussion. By helping our students to become more critical readers of problems, we enable them to gain insight into the problems and to begin to form their own way of solving problems.

8. Involve your students in both the problem and the process.

One way to motivate children to want to solve problems is to write problems about the children themselves. In fact, some teachers report the greatest success when children write their own textbook, complete with sets of problems about themselves and their classmates. Interest runs high as the children write story problems about their own everyday activities. They research supermarket prices, restaurant menus, the cost of toys, and so on.

ACTIVITY   Have groups of students collect and make up problems about themselves and their classmates that involve reasoning and mathematics appropriate to their grade level. The best of these can be illustrated by the students, then bound or stapled together to form a class problem-book. Duplicate the booklet so each child can have his or her own copy. Some of the problems may be based on material the students are studying in their other subjects, such as social studies and English.

     We also wish to involve the students actively in the solution process. Let students act out the problems. Involve them in activities such as surveys and shopping expeditions. Have them record their own data. Let them experiment!

PROBLEM   How high can you jump?
Who is the highest jumper in your class?

PROBLEM   How many M & M candies are there in 1 pound? How many of these are yellow? How many are red? Which color occurs the most?

PROBLEM   Which letter of the alphabet occurs most often in the first names of the children in your class?

PROBLEM   How fast can you roll a marble across the tray on the chalkboard in your classroom?

PROBLEM   How many times can you bounce a basketball in 1 minute?

Notice that these problems allow the children to actually get into the problem. They become a part of the story. Out come stopwatches, packages of candy, basketballs, and so on. The entire class becomes actively engaged in the problem-solving process.

PROBLEM   Three boys stood on a scale and put a nickel in the slot. The scale showed 205 pounds as their total weight. Two of the boys weigh the same. One boy stepped off the scale and it now showed 140 pounds. Find the weight of each of the boys.

Discussion   In class, you could ask three boys to act out this problem. When all three boys are standing "on the scale," show a sign that reads 205 pounds. Have one boy "step off." Now show a sign that reads 140 pounds. Notice that there are two possible answers to the problem, namely 65, 70, and 70 or 65, 65, and 75.

PROBLEM   How many empty soda cans can you put in a bag?

PROBLEM   What is the favorite sport chosen by the teachers in your school?

PROBLEM   When we eat a banana, an orange, and 1 peanut, how much do we actually eat? How much gets thrown away?

Discussion   The students can use a scale to weigh each of the items—first as we buy them in the store, and then after removing the shell or peel. If they cannot weigh exactly 1 peanut, help them arrive at the concept of weighing 10 peanuts and then taking $\frac{1}{10}$ weight.

9. Introduce manipulatives and drawings into the solution process.

Simulating the action by means of manipulatives or drawings is a bit more sophisticated than acting out the problem. It is the intermediate step between physically performing the action and solving the problem with symbols. The use of manipulatives and drawings permits the child to "see" what is taking place and to observe relationships that exist. The use of manipulatives should continue throughout the classroom work, and they should be readily available whenever students wish to use them. The manipulatives and/or drawings are used to simulate the activity portrayed in the problem. Drawings need not be exact in their representation, but they must be neat, accurate, and carefully drawn. Students must draw carefully labeled diagrams. Perpendiculars should look as if they form 90° angles; equal lengths should be drawn approximately equal. Directions should be carefully indicated.

This also means that the teacher must serve as a model for the students. When drawing diagrams at the board, make them carefully, but without the use of tools that differ from those the students might use. Practice in making freehand drawings is essential, since few teachers are so artistically inclined that they can draw well the first few times they attempt freehand drawings.

PROBLEM The circus is having a parade at the fairgrounds. There are 24 elephants in the parade. The ringmaster wants to arrange the elephants so that they will be in rows with the same number of elephants in each row. How many different ways can he do this?

Discussion Since it would be impractical to obtain 24 elephants to act out this problem, manipulatives such as bottle caps, chips, or small blocks would be suitable replacements. Children should note that 24 elephants in 1 row is not the same as 24 rows, each containing 1 elephant. This could lead to the difference between rows and columns in an array. In order not to count the same arrangement twice, and to be sure that all possibilities have been included, a table can be used to keep track of the different arrangements. In fact, the children might be introduced to an orderly approach by taking 1 row of 24, 2 rows of 12, 3 rows of 8, and so on. The resulting table:

Number of rows	Number of elephants in each row
1	24
2	12
3	8
4	6
6	4
8	3
12	2
24	1

The table clearly reveals that there are exactly 8 ways to arrange the 24 elephants.

PROBLEM There are some people seated around a circular picnic table. A plate of 15 cookies is passed around. Each person takes one cookie and then passes the plate on to the next person. Amrit takes the first cookie, and she also gets the last one. How many people were at the table?

Discussion This problem lends itself to a simulation with 15 chips or bottle caps. Reasoning tells us that there must be fewer than 15 people at the table, since Amrit took both the first and the last cookie.

Now act the problem out with 14 students. It works! But is this the *only* answer? Methodically try 13, 12, 11, . . 1 students. The correct answers are 1, 2, 7, and 14 people could have been seated at the table. Why?

PROBLEM Mr. Rosen, the music teacher, is arranging the chairs on stage for the chorale. He puts the chairs in the shape of a triangle, with 5 rows. The first row has 1 chair, the second row has 2 chairs. Each of the next rows contains as many seats as there are in all the rows in front of it. If there are exactly enough chairs for the members of the choir, how many members are there?

Discussion This is another problem that can be solved by using chips, markers, bottle caps, etc. The children should set up the 5 rows. They will discover that there are 1 + 2 + 3 + 6 + 12 or 24 chairs in the triangular array. Since there is a 1-to-1 correspondence between chorus members and chairs, the answer to the problem is 24 people in the choir.

PROBLEM Figure 3-4 shows a map of a small section of the city. Billy lives at the corner of Apple and 1st Streets. His school is at the corner of 3rd and Canteloupe Streets. All the straight lines represent one-way streets, as shown by the arrows (north or east). How many different paths can Billy's mother take when she drives Billy to school?

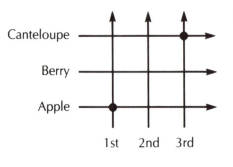

Figure 3–4

Discussion It is necessary to discuss with the children the meaning of the phrase "different paths." The children should use the drawing to trace each possible path for Billy's mother to take from their home to Billy's school. There are 6 different paths possible. Using a drawing reveals the answer more readily than any other procedure.

PROBLEM Paul Bunyan can cut a large log into 5 pieces in just 20 seconds. At the same rate, how long would it take him to cut the log into 10 pieces?

Discussion A drawing reveals that it takes 4 cuts to obtain 5 pieces, or five seconds per cut. Thus, it will take 9 cuts (or 45 seconds) to obtain 10 pieces.

ACTIVITY Distribute a series of problem situations that can be described by a drawing. Have each student make a drawing to illustrate the action. Discuss the drawings they have made. *Example:* Paula walked 5 blocks due north from her house. She then walked 4 blocks due east, and then 5 blocks due south. How many blocks is she from her home by the shortest path? The drawing in Figure 3–5 illustrates the problem setting and reveals that the figure formed is a rectangle.

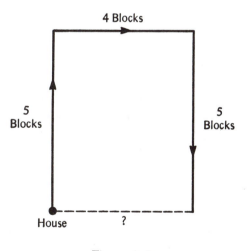

Figure 3–5

10. Suggest alternatives when students have been thwarted in their solution efforts.

It often happens that a student has no idea how to start the solution to a problem, or that a chosen strategy fails to provide an answer. Good problem solvers do not get discouraged! Instead, they persevere and continue their thinking or seek an alternative path. Many students, however, continue with the same approach even if it does not yield an answer. This is a predisposing condition or mindset that usually leads to the same end over and over again, by blocking out any kind of variable behavior. This mind-set must be changed and some other approach undertaken if the student has not successfully resolved the problem. The teacher should guide additional exploration by pointing out facts and inferences that might have been overlooked. Other suggestions can be made, as well. Guide, but don't take over!!

PROBLEM   How many squares are there on a 3-inch by 3-inch checkerboard as shown in Figure 3–6 ?

Figure 3–6

Discussion   Many students will quickly answer "Nine." Even if they are told that this is not the final answer, they often respond by counting the nine 1-inch squares that are most obvious in the figure. At this point, you should point out that the entire board is also a square, and then ask if there are squares of any other sizes on the checkerboard.

PROBLEM   Janina has a piece of wood that is 32 inches long. She cuts off an 11-inch piece. How many 3-inch pieces can she make from the wood she has left?

Discussion   Students will often divide 32 by 3 and give an answer of $10\frac{2}{3}$ pieces. Others will make a drawing to represent the 32-inch piece of wood and mark off 3-inch pieces. It may be necessary for you to point out that the problem will not work unless the 11-inch piece is *first* removed from the 32-inch piece of wood.

PROBLEM   June bought a candy bar for 30¢, and then sold it to Bobby for 40¢. She decided that she was still hungry, so she bought it back for 50¢. She again changed her mind and sold it to Lorna for 60¢. Did June gain money, lose money, or just break even?

Discussion   The students' immediate reaction would be that June just broke even. At this point, you could suggest that they act out the problem, regarding each pair of transactions separately.

PROBLEM   Mitch's Bike Shop ordered bicycles and tricycles for their stock. The shipment arrived unassembled. The box labeled "WHEELS" contained 23 wheels, and the box labeled "SEATS" contained 10 seats. How many bicycles and how many tricycles did Mitch order?

Discussion   How do we begin? Some students may have no idea! The 10 seats tell us that there were a total of 10 trikes and bikes altogether. We need only consider the 23 wheels in combinations of 2's and 3's. You might suggest that the students use 23 chips or markers to simulate the wheels. If further help is needed, you can suggest that they place the chips in piles of 2's and 3's. (There are 7 bicycles and 3 tricycles in the shipment).

When students are stuck, you might suggest that they look back at other problems they have solved in the past that were similar to the problem under consideration. This might lead to some ideas of what to do. Even a suggestion as to what might be done at a particular point is sometimes in order. Thus, you could suggest to students that one of the following might be a good idea to try:

1. Act it out.
2. Use manipulatives.
3. Make a drawing.
4. Look for a similar problem whose solution they already know.
5. Make a guess and check it.
6. Try a simpler version of the problem.
7. Make a table.
8. Use a calculator.
9. Work backwards from the answer.
10. Look for a pattern.
11. Divide the problem into several parts and solve each.
12. Use logical thinking.

Even encouraging students simply to pause and reflect carefully on the problem is a good technique to try when students are totally stymied.

11. Develop pupil skills in estimation.

Estimation is an important skill in many professions and vacations and in daily living. The development of students' ability to estimate should be an ongoing process. It takes time! Repeated exposure to estimating will build this skill and the children will gain the confidence necessary for accurate estimation. School mathematics, particularly with the use of the hand-held calculator, is a convenient place to help the students develop this needed skill. Estimation involves thinking that permits the student to conceptualize what is going on. That is, it permits us to hold off exact calculations until we know what is happening. We make the numbers easier to work with until we fully understand the problem.

Estimation goes beyond computational estimation, and includes estimating quantities and measurements as well. Students should be capable of:

exploring estimation strategies
recognizing when and where estimation is appropriate
using estimation to determine the reasonableness of results.

Estimation is not a simple process. Constant use of estimation will fortify the skill.

Estimation basically takes place in two areas: computational estimation and measurement estimation. Under computational, we include number sense as well as ordinary computation. Under measurement, we include length, weight, capacity, time, etc.

ACTIVITY

Prepare a sheet of "Is It Reasonable?" problems for the students. They are not to solve the problems. Rather, they are to decide if the answer given is reasonable. Here are some samples you might use:

1. The New York Giants and the New England Patriots are playing a football game. There are 69,782 people in the stadium. Tickets for the game averaged $11.65 each. About how much money was collected from ticket sales?
   Answer: About $70,000 was collected. (Not reasonable—there will be more than $700,000.)
2. There were 194,493 fans in attendance at the 4-game series between the New York Yankees and the Oakland Athletics. About how many people were at each game?
   Answer: There were about 50,000 fans at each game. (Reasonable.)
3. A cog railroad makes 24 round trips each day up the side of a mountain. On Monday, a total of 1,427 people rode

the cog railroad. About how many people rode on each trip?

Answer: About 60 people rode on each trip. (Reasonable.)

4. A hurricane is moving northward at the rate of 19 miles per hour. The storm is 95 miles south of Galveston. Approximately how long will it take the hurricane to reach Galveston?

Answer: It will take the storm about 5 minutes to reach Galveston. (Not reasonable—it will take approximately 5 *hours,* not 5 minutes.)

5. Mitchell jogged $\frac{1}{2}$ mile on Monday, $\frac{3}{8}$ mile on Tuesday, $\frac{5}{8}$ mile on Wednesday, $\frac{1}{2}$ mile on Thursday, and $\frac{3}{8}$ mile on Friday. About how many miles did he jog during the 5 days?

Answer: He jogged about 5 miles. (Not reasonable—the fractions are all close to $\frac{1}{2}$ mile. Thus the estimate should be about $2\frac{1}{2}$ miles.)

6. Mrs. O'Neill drove 683 miles and used 33 gallons of gasoline. About how many miles per gallon did she get?

Answer: She got about 40 miles per gallon. (Not reasonable—the trip was about 700 miles; she used about 35 gallons of gasoline, or about 20 miles per gallon.)

7. During the baseball season, 35,112 fans went to a Red Sox–Yankees game one Sunday; 27,982 fans saw the Phillies–Braves game that same day. About how many more fans were at the Red Sox–Yankees game?

Answer: About 700 more fans were at the Red Sox–Yankees game. (Not reasonable—it should be about 7,000.)

PROBLEM

1. Which has the largest value?

(a) 38 + 15
(b) 38 − 15
(c) 38 × 15
(d) 38 ÷ 15

2. Which has the largest value?

(a) .038 + .0015
(b) .038 − .0015
(c) .038 × .0015
(d) .038 ÷ .0015

Discussion

In number 1, multiplication gives the largest value, (c). In number 2, division gives the largest value, (d).

ACTIVITY

Estimate the time it would take you to do each of the following. Then check your estimate and see how close you came.

(a) Walk 100 yards.
(b) Dribble a basketball 50 times.
(c) Write the alphabet twice.
(d) Ride a bike from your home to your school.
(e) Walk completely around your classroom.
(f) Count the number of students in your class.

ACTIVITY   Ask the students to close their eyes and guess how long a minute is. Check them with a clock. See if they can come within 15 seconds, then within 10 seconds, then within 5 seconds. Have them record how close they come each time.

ACTIVITY   Find a book with a large number of pages. Note the number of pages in the book. Place a bookmark anywhere in the book. Have the students look at the bookmark and guess the number of the page it is marking. Try this several times. Have students keep a record of how many times their guesses were within 10 pages of the bookmark.

ACTIVITY   Have the students look closely at the classroom. Have them estimate its length, its width, and its height. Check the student guesses by having them actually measure as much as they can, using a tape measure, yardstick, or other measuring device.

ACTIVITY   How many paper clips high are you? How many paper clips long is your classroom?

Drawings can also be used to provide students with practice in estimation skills. Figures 3–7 through 3–10 will give the students an opportunity to estimate. In each case, students should be aware that they must establish a reference base.

ACTIVITY   Send your class on an Estimation Scavenger Hunt. This can be done either in school, or on their way to and from school, as a homework assignment.
See how many of the following you can find.

a. Something that is about 5 feet long.
b. Something that weighs about 20 pounds.
c. A book that is about 3 inches thick.
d. A picture that is about 11-inches by 14 inches.
e. A circle that has a diameter of about 12 inches.
f. An equilateral triangle whose side is about 18 inches.
g. A container that can hold about 20 gallons.

This jar contains 10
ounces of oil.

How many ounces
of oil does this jar
contain?

(Answer: Approximately 20 ounces)

Figure 3-7

The tightrope walker has walked 20 feet.
How many more feet must he walk to
reach the other side?

(Answer: Approximately 40 feet more)

Figure 3–8

ACTIVITY   In each case, decide whether an estimate is sufficient, or an
exact answer is needed.

1. A clerk is figuring out the sales tax on a person's purchase.
   (Exact)
2. An airline passenger wants to know what time a particular flight leaves. (Exact)
3. Television viewers are interested in the size of the crowd
   at the presidential inauguration. (Estimate)

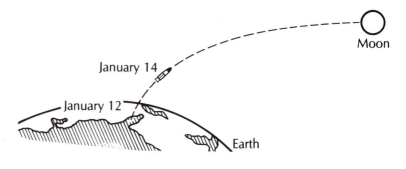

The rocket blasted off from Earth on January 12.
Estimate the date it will arrive on the moon.

(Answer: Approximately January 20)

Figure 3–9

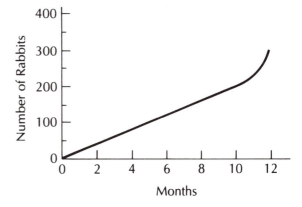

From the graph, estimate the number
of rabbits at the end of 12 months.

(Answer: Approximately 300 rabbits)

Figure 3–10

4. Sandra has a doctor's appointment at 7:00 P.M. She can walk 1 block in 3 minutes and has 12 blocks to walk. At what time should she leave her home for the appointment? (Exact)
5. A homeowner is figuring out how much paint he needs to paint the garage. (Estimate)

6. An air tank permits a diver to stay underwater for 1 hour. Marcella's tank is $\frac{3}{4}$ full. How long can she stay underwater? (Estimate)

ACTIVITY   *Making Sense* is an activity for a small group of students, to help them improve their estimation skills. A paragraph of several sentences is presented, describing a situation in which several numbers are used. However, blanks are inserted where the numbers were, and the numbers are mixed up in a separate row. The problem is to fit the numbers where they most probably belong, to "make sense" of the paragraph.

Example: Pauline , _____ years old, just set a new record for eating chocolate chip cookies. She ate _____ cookies in just _____ minutes. This set a new record by just _____ cookies.

7,   100,   227,   2

(The correct order is 7, 227, 100, 2.)

Example: In Reading, a local newspaper offered _____ families a chance to be part of the study. If they were accepted, each family would receive $ _____ and would have to give up television watching for _____ months. Only _____ familes applied for the study.

1,000   112,   2,   7

(The correct order is 112,   1000,   2,   7.)

Example: The restaurant on top of a New York City hotel is about _____ feet high. It revolves completely through _____ degrees every _____ minutes. The restaurant is open _____ hours per day.

60,   8,   360,   440

(The correct order is 440,   360,   60,   8.)

ACTIVITY   Have the students prepare a list of activities in which they engage during a typical day. Include such items as waking up in the morning, meal times, leaving for school, homework, television time, and other pastimes. Tell for which of these events they need exact times or if an estimate will do. Tell why and give specific illustrations.

Activities such as these will help students improve their ability to estimate accurately.

12. Encourage students to make conjectures.

Conjecturing is the act of sensing or guessing the outcome of a situation. It is often a brainstorming activity that produces predictions that may be quickly rejected or modified. The result should lead to a probable generalization

When your students are confronted by a problem that must be resolved, they analyze the data, organize it, and make inferences. At some point, they will come up with a "hunch," a possible pattern, or a conjecture.

An open classroom environment is necessary for conjecturing to take place. Too often the teacher, in a desire to draw closure on a problem, steps in too soon with the "correct" procedure or answer. At this point, the conjecturing ends. Nothing more can be learned. Many times it is better to let the conjecturing continue, along with the associated verification procedures.

PROBLEM Are there more prime numbers between 1 and 99, or between 100 and 199 ?

Discussion Students might conjecture that there are more prime numbers in the first 100 numbers. They should then decide upon a plan to prove or disprove their conjecture.

PROBLEM Are there more whole numbers than even numbers?

Discussion Most people would intuitively conjecture that there are more whole numbers than even numbers. Let's attempt to validate this conjecture. This might be done by making a list of the even numbers and counting them, putting them into a one-to-one correspondence with the counting numbers:

$$
\begin{array}{ccccc}
2 & 4 & 6 & 8 & 10 \quad \ldots \\
\downarrow & \downarrow & \downarrow & \downarrow & \downarrow \\
1 & 2 & 3 & 4 & 5 \quad \ldots
\end{array}
$$

96

In this way, the children see that the conjecture is not valid, since, for every even number, there is a corresponding whole number. (This, of course, is only true because of the fact that both are infinite sets.)

PROBLEM   Each of 3 differently shaped containers (as shown in Figure 3-11) is filled with 8 ounces of water on Monday. By Friday, which will have lost the most water by evaporation?

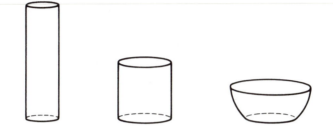

Figure 3–11

Discussion   Have the students make their conjectures and discuss their reasoning. Then have them suggest ways in which they might verify their conjectures.

13. Have students reflect on their own thought processes.

When a problem has been solved and an answer arrived at and checked, the attention of the students should be focused on what reasoning actually took place. Individual students should carefully reflect and consider what they did, why they did it, and how they did it. At this point, they should share their thinking with the rest of the class. These metacognitive thoughts should be discussed, since they will form the foundation for good reasoning patterns for resolving future problems.

Another technique for achieving these goals is to have students write a *summary paragraph* of their thought processes at the conclusion of each problem solution. These paragraphs will help students in their communication skills as well.

An additional way to encourage reflective thinking, one that is beneficial in its own right, is to have the children flowchart the thinking process they have just used to resolve a problem situation. In order to construct a flow chart, the child must reflect on the process that he or she has just gone through in a step-by-step fashion, thus producing the kind of reflective thought that we are seeking to develop. A typical flow chart might look like the one in Figure 3–12 on page 99.

The preparation of a flow chart is an extremely valuable procedure for both student and teacher. It helps students to reflect on their thought processes. It can also serve as a model for future problem-solving and reasoning activities. For the teacher, it provides an opportunity to examine the thought processes the students have developed. It is a visual example of what the students were thinking as they attempted to solve the problem.

Some people suggest that students keep a *metacognitive journal*, writing down their thought processes as they take place in the attempts to solve a problem. It is our feeling that keeping a metacognitive journal while solving the problem may interfere with the natural flow of the problem-solving process, inhibiting creativity and conjecturing. We would prefer that these reflective acts be done after the problem situation has been resolved, i.e., as in a summary paragraph.

14. Require your students to create their own problems.

If we asked students where problems come from, they would most likely answer that they come "from the textbook" or "from the teacher." Thus, problems are simply activities posed by the teacher, which they, the students, are required to solve. They see little relationship between problems they do in their mathematics classroom and the problems they face in their everyday living. When students write their own problems or ask significant questions about a problem situation, they begin to see that situation in a new light and with deeper understanding. We suggest that students should initiate problems and questions, that they should engage in creative, mathematical thinking.

Nothing helps children become better problem solvers than having to make up their own problems. In order to create a problem, the student must know the ingredients. They must relate setting, facts, questions, and distractors. We know that children create excellent problems. In fact, their problems are usually more relevant (and often more complex) than the ones typically found in their textbooks.

An easy and effective technique for starting children as problem creators is to provide them with answers for which they must write appropriate problems.

Example: The answer is 6. What's the problem?

At first, the children may offer such questions as, "How much is 4 + 2?" or "How much is 12 ÷ 2?" However, if the teacher responds with, "You can do better than that. Make it more interesting," more complex story problems will result. This idea should be expanded to include such answers as 5 feet, 18 pounds, $9.12, 16 girls and 4 boys, etc.

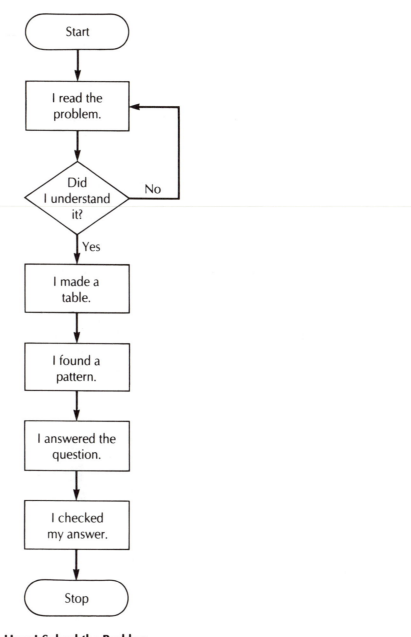

How I Solved the Problem

Figure 3–12

A higher level of sophistication can be achieved by directing the students, "Write a problem whose answer is 8 and that involves subtraction." Additional conditions can be added by supplying a setting for the problem as well.

Example: Write a problem set in the museum gift shop, where the answer is $5.00 and the problem involves addition.

ACTIVITY   Show some pictures that have been taken from old magazines, old catalogs, old textbooks, etc. Have the students make up a story problem to fit each picture.

Discussion   This activity helps students learn to decide on numerical data that make sense, for they must use realistic numbers in designing their problem. At the same time, this activity helps students to integrate mathematical problems with their other subjects, such as social studies, language arts, and science.

ACTIVITY   Distribute several drawings that illustrate problem situations. Have your students make up a problem for which the given drawing is appropriate. Discuss these problems with the entire class.
Example: Although the problems that the students will create may vary, here is one possible problem suggested by the drawing in Figure 3–13:

Figure 3–13

"At the end of the day, Clarice put all of her money on the kitchen table. She had a $1 bill, 4 dimes, and 3 nickels. How much money did she have?"

Example: one problem that a student might create from the drawing in Figure 3–14 is:

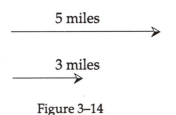

Figure 3–14

"One movie theater is 5 miles from Gregory's house. The second movie theater is 3 miles from his house in the same direction. How far apart are the two theaters?"

ACTIVITY   Ask your students to write a menu problem. That is, given the menu shown in Figure 3–15, write a problem about it.

Hot dog	.95
Hamburger	1.55
Grilled chicken breast	2.05
Pizza (per slice)	.95
Tuna sandwich	1.85
Grilled cheese sandwich	1.35
Apple	.25
Banana	.35
Milk (white)	.35
Milk (chocolate)	.45
Candy Bar	2 for .75

Figure 3–15

Discussion   At first, many students will probably write problems that merely list an order of 2 or more items from the menu and then ask for their total cost. A higher level of problem may be given by some students in which the amount of change from a large bill is asked for. A third-level problem might involve stating the total amount spent and asking about what could have been purchased. (Students may be surprised when multiple answers appear.) Adding tax may complicate the problem even further.

As the students gain experience in creating their own problems, the problems will become more sophisticated. There will be some with insufficient information and some with excess information. This is highly desirable because the problem-solving process is what should be stressed. Problems that appear in textbooks often emphasize one particular skill or operation. On the other hand, these student-generated problems frequently involve extraneous data and possibly more than one operation. Some examples of student problems with insufficient or excess information follow.

PROBLEM   My mother, father, sister, and I went to the local pizza restaurant. We ate 2 pizzas. How many slices did my sister eat?

PROBLEM   On Tuesday, Mrs. Kwan went to the supermarket. She bought 2 pounds of tomatoes at $1.85 a pound, and 3 pounds of bananas at 69¢ a pound. She gave the clerk a $10 bill. How much did she spend?

PROBLEM   An ostrich egg weighs about 48 ounces. How many chicken eggs would it take to weigh this much?

PROBLEM   Sol had a 48-inch length of wood. He cut off a piece to use for a sign. His dad cut the rest into 2 parts to use for shelves. How long was each shelf?

PROBLEM   Cindy answered 3 questions correctly on her math test. How many questions did she get wrong?

PROBLEM   According to the local weather station, we had 20.2 cm of rain by the tenth of April. By the fifteenth of April, this number had risen to 22.9 cm. The rainfall for the entire month was 23.7 cm. How much rain fell between the fifteenth and the thirtieth of April?

ACTIVITY   Supply both the work and the answer. Ask students to write the problem. For example,

1. $\dfrac{75° + 80° + 98° + 91°}{4}$ The answer is 86°

$$2. \quad 45 \overline{)225} \quad 5$$

$$\begin{array}{r} 225 \\ \underline{225} \\ 0 \end{array}$$

The answer is 5 hours.

Select several students to present their problems to the class. Have the entire class solve the problems. Sharing problems that have been written by other students should be an integral part of your classroom procedure. The fact that the problems have been designed by classmates usually heightens interest in solving them. These problems may simply be variations of other problems that students have seen, or they may be entirely original creations. In any case, they are always interesting to other students.

15. Use strategy games in class.

There is no real satisfaction in winning a strategy game if the person wins because his or her opponent made a foolish move or a mistake. Rather, the real enjoyment in winning occurs when a tentative strategy is developed, moves and countermoves are made and examined, and a general strategy that will win all or most of the time evolves.

Research has shown that children who are guided in playing strategy games usually improve their reasoning and problem-solving abilities. That is, children who are good problem solvers, usually are good strategy game players, and vice versa. This section discusses the use of these games as a vehicle for developing problem-solving and reasoning skills. These are *not* games that necessarily involve arithmetic skills (although they might). Rather, to be considered a strategy game, the game must meet the following conditions:

1. The game must have a definite set of rules for the players.
2. The game should be played by at least two players, each of whom has a goal; these goals must be in conflict with one another.
3. Each player must make intelligent choices of moves, based on whatever information is available at the time of the move.
4. Each player tries to stop the opponent from achieving his or her goal before achieving his or her own goal.

Notice that luck or sheer chance should play a minimal role in strategy gaming.

Why games? First of all, games have a strong appeal for children and adults alike. We know that most people enjoy games. All one must do is examine the many books of puzzles and games that are sold in bookstores, or look at the puzzles and games that appear on napkins in restaurants or in magazines on airplanes. Currently, the personal computer is creating a new wave of strategy games, games with which children are becoming increasingly familiar. The game arcades in most major shopping centers and malls are indicative of this interest in games of *all* types.

Secondly, children have been exposed to games and gaming all of their lives. They have learned what a game is, that games are fun, that games have rules, and that it is often possible to win consistently at a particular game by developing an appropriate strategy. Most of your students are already familiar with strategy games such as checkers and chess; they already know basic strategies for these games.

To students, games are real-world reasoning situations. They want to win; they enjoy playing the games. Remember that skills acquired under enjoyable conditions are retained for longer periods of time than are skills acquired under stress or other adverse conditions.

When children try to develop a strategy for winning at a strategy game, they usually go through a reasoning process that consists of a series of steps, closely paralleling those used in problem solving

1. Read the game rules. Understand the play of the game. Analyze the game. What is a move? What pieces are involved? What does the board look like? What constitutes a win? When is a game over?
2. Correlate the rules with those from any related game. Is there a similar game whose strategy you already know? Conjecture. Select several possible lines of play to follow in an attempt to win the game.
3. Carry out a selected line of play. Can you counter your opponent's moves as the game proceeds? Does your strategy produce a win?
4. Look back at the game. Reflect. If your strategy produced a win, will it work every time? If your strategy did not produce a win, why not? Could you modify your original strategy? Try alternative lines of play, alternative moves.

The similarity between this sequence and the sets of heuristics we described in Chapter 2 is indeed marked.

In order to use strategy games effectively with your students, you need a large selection and a wide variety of games. These games can be found in many places. Best of all, games already known to the students can be varied by changing the rules, the pieces, or the game board. In these cases, students need not spend an inordinate amount of time learning all about a new game, but can immediately move to developing a strategy for play. For example, most of your students already know the game of Tic-Tac-Toe. Under the usual rules, the player who first gets three of his or her own marks (usually X and O) in a straight line either vertically, horizontally, or diagonally, is the *winner*. A simple rule change might be to decide that the first player who gets three of his or her marks in a straight line is the *loser*. This creates an entirely new line of play and requires a different analysis and strategy of play.

When you use these games with your students, have them analyze and discuss their play. Have them keep a record of their moves in each game. You can help them in this analysis by asking key questions, such as:

1. Do I know what I must do to win?
2. Is it a good idea for me to go first?
3. Should I play a defensive game (that is, react to your opponent's moves) or an offensive game?
4. If I won, was it just luck or could I use the same strategy to win the next time?
5. Can I describe my strategy in words so that other students can use it? Does it work for them, too?

Have students play each game several times, refining their strategy each time they play. Discuss with the class those strategies that consistently lead to a win. Help students follow the reasoning process behind the winning strategies. Follow the strategy gaming process with the children.

You can find many examples of commercial strategy games by browsing through a local toy store or by examining the many collections of games available in bookstores. To get you started, a collection of strategy games has been suggested in Section A.

16. Take advantage of computer programming.

An increasing number of schools are including courses in computer literacy, awareness, and programming in their curriculum. The programming of a computer draws on many of the skills used in problem solving and reasoning. When students are asked to write a program, they must analyze the task at hand, draw on their previous knowledge and experiences, and put together an organized plan of steps, operations, and commands that yield the correct results. This format of a program is very much like the heuristics pattern of reasoning and problem solving. Several languages can be used, such as LOGO, BASIC, etc. We have used the BASIC language in the programs that follow.

PROBLEM   Tell what the output will be for each of the following programs.

(A) 10   LET A = 10

    20   LET B = 5 + 8

    30   LET C = A * B

    40   PRINT C

    50   END

(B) 10   LET R = 5 - 2

    20   LET S = 16 + 4

    30   LET T = 9 * R

    40   PRINT R + S

    50   END

Discussion   An activity such as this provides students with the opportunity to analyze a sequence of steps. This is a skill similar to that needed in analyzing problems. Notice that line 30 in (b) is excess information; it does not affect the output.

PROBLEM   Put line numbers in the following program so that it will print out the perimeter of a rectangle.

```
LET P = 2 * L + 2 * W
LET L = 14.6
START
END
PRINT "THE PERIMETER IS "; P
LET W = 10.8
```

Discussion   This exercise provides the students with practice in ordering the steps in a given sequence. Each step must be placed within the program so as to follow in a logical order.

PROBLEM   Write a program for finding the area of a rectangle, given its length and width.

Discussion   In order to do this, the student must know what a program is, what a rectangle is, and what is meant by length, width, and area. In other words, he or she must understand what is being asked for and what is given. This is exactly the same as the first phase of the problem-solving process. Analysis is taking place. The student must now review his or her knowledge of areas and rectangles to find the proper formula. Now this information is synthesized and the program written. This carries the student through the solve phase of the heuristics. A sample result might be:

```
5    HOME
10   REM AREA OF A RECTANGLE
20   PRINT "TYPE IN THE LENGTH IN INCHES"
30   INPUT L
35   PRINT
40   PRINT "TYPE IN THE WIDTH IN INCHES"
50   INPUT W
55   PRINT:PRINT
60   LET A = L * W
70   PRINT "THE AREA OF THE RECTANGLE IS"; A; "SQUARE INCHES"
80   END
```

The student now runs the program. Does it work? (This is the Reflect phase). If not, why not? If it does run correctly, how could it be modified to extend it to other geometric figures? (Extend/ generalize.)

PROBLEM   Here is a program designed to find the average of 3 numbers. Some steps have been omitted. Supply the missing steps. Then run the program.

```
10   REM FINDING AVERAGES
20   INPUT A
30
40   INPUT C
50   LET S = A + B + C
60
70   PRINT "THE AVERAGE OF THE THREE NUMBERS IS"; M
80   END
```

Discussion   This program is an exact parallel to the problem-solving situation in which there is missing data. Being able to determine what information is required to resolve a problem situation and to supply such information assures us that the problem solver has a thorough understanding of the problem situation.

PROBLEM   Here is a program designed to tell you how much change you receive from a $10 bill when you make 3 purchases in a grocery store. Some steps have been omitted. Supply the missing steps. Then run the program.

```
10    REM CHANGE PROGRAM
20    PRINT "P IS WHAT YOU SPENT FOR POTATOES"
30    INPUT P
40    PRINT "B IS WHAT YOU SPENT FOR BANANAS"
50    INPUT B
60    PRINT "M IS WHAT YOU SPENT FOR MILK"
70    LET S = P + B + M
80    PRINT "YOUR CHANGE IS"; C
90    END
```

Discussion   This problem is similar to the previous one. However, it has an additional complexity; the missing steps have not been identified. The missing steps are:

```
65    INPUT M
75    LET C = 10 - S
```

(Note: The programs in this section have been written for the Apple microcomputer.)

17. Use the calculator as a learning aid.

A calculator should not be used as a substitute for learning the arithmetic algorithms. However, having learned the algorithms, students should feel free to use the calculator whenever *they* feel it is appropriate.

For the development of reasoning and problem-solving skills, the calculator can play an important role. It enables us to use problems with real-life data, because computation with these numbers is now feasible. We no longer have to rely on artificial situations where the numbers have been adjusted for easy computation to nice, neat answers. The student can feel free to focus on the problem and the reasoning it entails, without being overly concerned with the numerical computation he or she faces. The truth is, the calculator only plays a limited role in the development of problem-solving and reasoning skills, since its primary function is to simplify calculations.

PROBLEM   How many days have you lived? (Consider a year as having exactly 365 days.)

Discussion   The students will have to change the number of full years to days, and the remaining months to days. Answers, of course, will vary.

PROBLEM   Mrs. Robert s wanted to buy some grapefruit. Her local supermarket sells grapefruit at 2 for 59¢ or a bag of 10 for $2.78. What should she do?

Discussion   Ten grapefruit at 2 for 59¢ will cost $2.95. Thus she saves 17¢ by buying the bag of 10. However, if she does not need 10 grapefruit and some might spoil, she would be better off buying a smaller quantity.

PROBLEM   About how many words are there in your history book?

Discussion   Here is a problem that involves sampling, counting, and computation. The student might count the number of words on an "average" page in the book, then multiply by the number of pages. Or find the average number of words per page in a 5-page sample, and then multiply by the number of pages. What other ways can they suggest for finding the answer?

PROBLEM   The postage rate for a first-class letter in 1991 was 29¢ for the first ounce or fraction, and 23¢ for each additional ounce or fraction. If Marcie wants to mail a letter that weighs $7\frac{1}{2}$ ounces, how much postage does she need?

Discussion   Students should come to realize that $7\frac{1}{2}$ ounces requires the same amount of postage as does $7\frac{1}{4}$ ounces, $7\frac{3}{4}$ ounces, or any weight up to, but not including, 8 ounces. Thus we need 1 ounce at 29¢ and 7 additional ounces at 23¢.

PROBLEM   Using the digits 8, 7, 6, 5, and 4, what is the largest product you can form?

Discussion   Some children may decide to write a 4-digit number multiplied by a 1-digit number (for example, 8,765 × 4); others may write a 3-digit number multiplied by a 2-digit number (i.e., 654 × 87). Have students investigate all possible products, keeping track of each.

PROBLEM   The table below shows the population of 6 major cities in the United States. If the population of the United States was about 280,000,000 what percent of the people live in each of these 6 cities? In all 6 cities combined?

City	Population
New York	7,071,639
Chicago	3,005,072
Los Angeles	2,966,850
Houston	1,595,138
Philadelphia	1,688,210
Detroit	1,203,339

Discussion The data in this problem enable many questions to be asked and answered. We have chosen 2 that, by paper and pencil, would be awkward. However, the calculator makes all of them quite manageable.

18. Promote resourcefulness, creativity, and imagination.

Mathematics, problem solving, and reasoning must go beyond what usually appears in textbooks. Most mathematics lessons are devoted to finding the answers to specific questions or attaining algorithmic skill. If we are to develop thinking individuals, we must place them in situations that can only be resolved by applying resourcefulness, creativity, and imagination. These can be projects or activities that depart from what traditionally takes place in the classroom. Below are several representative activites that can be used to stimulate and challenge our students to think!!

ACTIVITY In science class, the children learned that some birds eat 6 times their own body weight every day. How long would it take *you* to eat an amount of food equal to your body-weight?

Discussion Have the children work in groups and develop a plan for answering this question. Since this is a new type of activity for most children, you may have to make some suggestions to get them started. For example, you could ask "how much do you think the food you ate for breakfast weighed?" "How much do you think the food you ate all day yesterday weighed?" (Don't forget snacks!) "How could you figure out the weight of the food you eat in 1 day? "(Three days?)" "How might you answer the question?" "Will your answer be exact or will an estimate suffice?"

ACTIVITY Kile came to school one day with 2 of his front teeth missing. Mr. Robinson, the kindergarten teacher, said to him, "This is a little bit early for teeth to fall out. You're a little young!" Which class in your school has the most missing teeth?

Discussion The children will have to conduct a survey of the classes in the school. How should they undertake the survey? Should they ask all the students or should they sample? Does the number of students in each class affect the answer? How should the data be organized and presented?

ACTIVITY Have the children play Adopt-a-Number. Each child selects a number to "adopt", i.e, 1, 6, 27, 83, etc. They then try to find their number in their everyday life. They might look at a ruler, auditorium seats, page numbers in their books, a magazine page, the time on the clock, etc. Each child can write about the places where his or her number was used. The person who found his or her number being used the most is the winner.

ACTIVITY Have children keep track of every place where they use numbers for a whole day. Be sure that they include such less-obvious places such as the channel numbers on their television set, their house number, the time they leave for school, classroom numbers, etc. Who can find the most uses for numbers?

ACTIVITY Traffic lights are supposed to remain red or green depending on the ratio of moving traffic in both directions at the intersection. Select a busy corner near your school. Find out if the timing of the traffic light is correct.

Discussion One way may be to provide each group of students with a stopwatch (or a watch with a sweep second hand) and a clipboard. Have them actually time the lights and count the number of cars. Work out the answer. See if it is actually a proportion.

ACTIVITY "Boy," said Jerry's dad, "all this junk mail we get every day must cost someone a small fortune. if I only had the money that gets spent on sending us all our mail for a month, I bet I could buy us a new color television." If this happened in your house, if your dad said this, would he be right? How could you tell?

Discussion Students must first decide on the price for the color television. This has quite a range. Now, should the students keep count for a full month? Or can they sample? How should they sample? One day a week? One whole week? Several days? Which days? (More mail *comes* on different days of the month.)

ACTIVITY   The class is trying to find out what part of a typical hour of television time is spent on commercials. They guessed that this would vary depending on the time of day, the day of the week, and the channel. Is their guess correct?

Discussion   Different groups of children will suggest different ways of solving this problem. Don't forget to check Saturday mornings.

ACTIVITY   Each bill of paper money that we use has a letter in the lower right hand corner of the bill. This letter tells us from which city the bill comes. There are federal banks that issue money in the following 12 cities:

A = Boston	E = Richmond	I = Minneapolis
B = New York	F = Atlanta	J = Kansas City
C = Philadelphia	G = Chicago	K= Dallas
D = Cleveland	H = St. Louis	L = San Francisco

Find the letter designation on a bill. Then look at 10 bills chosen at random. List the number of bills that come from each bank. Combine your totals with those of 9 other classmates. Were all 12 banks represented in your results? Why did this happen?

ACTIVITY   How many times can you fold a piece of paper? Take a large piece of paper and fold it in half. Now fold it in half again. Continue folding it in half. How many times were you able to fold it? What if you chose a much thinner piece of paper?

Discussion   Students may be surprised at the small number of times they can fold a piece of paper. Even with a large sheet of very thin paper, the number of times will be quite small.

A WORD ABOUT ASSESSMENT

Traditional tests have been fairly effective in measuring the achievement level of students in the areas of algorithms or memorized facts and procedures. However, we are now being confronted by a different assessment task. Assessing students' working knowledge of higher-order thinking skills is a far different procedure. Traditional paper and pencil, objective-type tests will not do the entire job. Process skills such as problem solving and reasoning require additional forms of testing.

Many mathematics educators are now attempting to develop ways to assess student achievement of higher-order thinking skills. However, even before these measures become readily available, you, the classroom teacher, are responsible for evaluation and diagnosis of student progress in these areas. To help in this task, we need a variety of performance-oriented assessment tools. Some will be oral, some will involve written presentations, some will include observations, and some will be written tests.

You should maintain a portfolio for each of the students in your class. In this portfolio you should keep observation notes, the student's written work, project reports, test results, and so on. Even brief anecdotal comments should be placed in this portfolio.

1. Observations.

While the students are working on a problem in small groups, walk around the room, simply observing them in action. As they work in their groups, you move about the room, focusing your observations on some aspects of the situation that you feel are important. You may want to ask some informal questions, such as, "How did you do this?" "What made you try that?" "What do you think about your answer?" This observation technique enables you to work with selected students and observe them in action as they reason through a problem situation. You should make some mental notes of the students' behaviors as you move about the room. These should be written down right after class. Are the students willing to try to solve the problem? Do they work cooperatively in groups? Do they keep trying, even after they have experienced some trouble solving the problem? Do they demonstrate self-confidence? These notes will become a part of the student's portfolio.

Unfortunately, this technique of assessment has some disadvantages. First of all, it is time-consuming. You cannot possibly hope to observe all of your students every day. Secondly, record keeping can become overwhelming. Finally, it is often difficult to remain quiet when you see students "heading off in the wrong direction."

2. Metacognitive journals and summary paragraphs.

Helping students to think about their own thinking and to make changes in how they think is the essence of metacognition. We want our students to become better and better in this process as they engage in problem solving and reasoning. Many of these metacognitive ideas should be built into your lessons. We can encourage our students to think about their own thinking as they proceed, important for many reasons, but especially to help students rethink their own process, to make ongoing changes in their thinking patterns.

In one type of metacognitive journal, students each work a problem on the right-hand page of a two-page spread. On the left-side page, the students record what made them do what they did at each stage of the solution, concurrent with their actions. What did they do to get started? Why did they do it? What criteria did they use to make a choice of strategy? What happened if that initial strategy choice did not work? Was there a sudden flash of insight? What happened when they arrived at a tentative answer?

A second kind of metacognitive journal (and the one we prefer) is the same in appearance but is arrived at in a different manner. Here, the student completes the solution to the problem and *then* reflects on each step of the process, entering the data and commentary on the left-side page directly opposite the appropriate steps of the solution. As we have said before, this method does not disturb the natural flow of thinking during the actual solution process.

In a summary paragraph, the same considerations are included as in a metacognitive journal. However, this is a single paragraph, written after the solution has been completed, and not concurrent with every step.

The metacognitive journal and summary paragraph are ideas that have been used by many elementary school teachers in a variety of subject areas, yet they are rarely used as assessment tools in mathematics. If our students are used to writing about their daily experiences in a journal, it should be natural for them to do the same in mathematics. Students can be asked to write ideas and feelings in their journals; these will often provide a great deal of insight into our learning what the student's thinking is. Whenever our students begin to think about their own thinking, they begin to do much more conscious thinking!

By examining these journals, we get a better picture of how students are using the problem-solving process. Are they better organized in their approaches? Have they selected and used a variety of strategies? Do they look for patterns? What happens when they find themselves stuck? In all cases, we can obtain a better picture of the students' knowledge of the reasoning and problem-solving processes.

3. Tests.

a. Multiple-choice tests. Although we have previously said that most multiple-choice tests are ineffective in assessing higher-order thinking skills, there are some kinds of multiple-choice questions that can be useful. For example, we might wish to assess how well children can interpret the action of a problem, the understanding of a question, or the ability to read a problem and estimate the answer. Here are some sample questions you might consider.

PROBLEM   Luis is permitted to watch 16 hours of television each week. If he watched 8 hours on the weekend, how many hours can he watch television during the week?
Which of the following statements is true?

(a)   The problem deals with the kinds of television programs Luis can watch.
(b)   The problem deals with the amount of time that Luis can watch television during the week.
(c)   The problem deals with the amount of homework that Luis is required to do before he can watch television.

PROBLEM   Ariel and Kermit went fishing from 8:00 A.M. to 3:30 P.M. They caught 7 flounder, 2 sea bass and 3 weakfish. How many fish did they catch altogether?
Which of the following answers the question being asked in the problem?

(a)   They fished for $7\frac{1}{2}$ hours.
(b)   They caught 3 different kinds of fish.
(c)   They caught 7 flounder.
(d)   They caught 12 fish.

PROBLEM   A robot paints 6 car doors in one hour. Last week, the robot worked for 40 hours. Which of the following is the best estimate of the number of car doors the robot painted last week?

(a) 6   (b) 250   (c) 1000

b. Open-ended questions. Posing open-ended questions is another technique that teachers use to help assess critical and creative thinking. By an open-ended question, we mean one that requires the child to think creatively, requires a written response, and permits the teacher to examine the thought process that was used.

PROBLEM   Geordie and Juan bought a large sandwich that they were going to share for their lunch. They cut the sandwich into 2 equal parts. Just as they were about to start eating, Louis arrived and announced that he had left his lunch at home. The 3 boys all agreed to share the sandwich equally. Explain how they could do this.

Discussion   A written response to this question permits us to examine the child's thinking. Read the child's solution carefully. Some of the things you should look for include:

1. Did the child arrive at a fair way of dividing the sandwich?
2. Did each person receive an equal share?
3. Was the explanation logical?
4. Did the student suggest more than one way to solve the problem?
5. Were these alternate ways correct?
6. Were the alternate explanations logical?

PROBLEM   Jesse, Janet, and Carl drove home from a weekend in the country. They took turns driving. Carl drove for 65 miles. Jesse drove for 42 miles. Janet drove twice as many miles as Carl. How long was the entire trip?
Michael said that the answer to this problem was 130 miles. Tell whether Michael's answer was right or wrong. Explain how you reached your decision.

PROBLEM   There are 20 people in line, waiting for the new music store to open. Each person was given a number from 1 through 20. Just before opening time, the store manager began passing out coupons good for free gifts. He gave coupons for a free cassette to the first person in line. Then he skipped 2 people and gave a coupon to the next person. He then skipped 2 more people and gave a coupon to the next person, and so on. The assistant manager came out next, and she gave a coupon for a free record brush to each of the people holding an odd number. How many people in the line did not receive coupons for a gift? How many for 1 gift? For 2 gifts? For 3 gifts?
How would you solve this problem? Give as many ways as possible. Explain each way.

c. *Performance tests*. This kind of test requires that the student solve a given problem completely and correctly. The ultimate goal in problem solving is to develop the skills necessary to solve a problem and get the correct answer. This type of test should be scored, traditionally with partial credit being given when a student demonstrates the proper direction, and full credit only given when the solution and the answer are both correct.

One thing which we must stress before we close this section, There is no one assessment device has proven to be sufficient by itself. If we wish to improve our teaching of reasoning and problem solving, then we must constantly assess both our own teaching and our students' progress in learning. Assessment becomes an on-going process, an integral part of the teaching-learning act. We must utilize a wide variety of techniques to assess each of our students. Although the process is indeed longer than merely giving a simple test and marking the answers right or wrong, we should utilize this wide variety of techniques to assess all parts of the reasoning process. If we wish to assess the effectiveness of our teaching, we must face up to the fact that there is no simple way to assess student progress.

SECTION A

A Collection
of Strategy Games

TIC–TAC–TOE VARIATIONS

The basic game of Tic-Tac-Toe is a good starting point for introducing strategy games to children. In many cases, your students will already be familiar with the rules of the game. Thus, it becomes a logical place to find a wide assortment of variations.

1. Tic-Tac-Toe

The game is played by two people on a nine-cell array as shown in Figure A–1. Give each player five chips, markers, or tokens of a distinctive color. Or assign X to one player and O to the other. The players alternate turns, placing one of their markers in any empty cell. The winner is the person who gets three in a row horizontally, vertically, or diagonally.

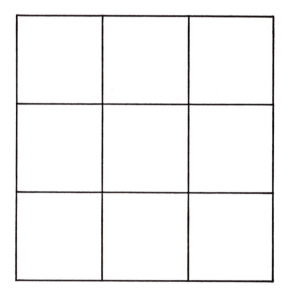

Figure A–1. Tic-Tac-Toe Game Board

2. Valley Tic-Tac-Toe

The game is played on an eight-cell board as shown in Figure A–2. Players take turns placing one of their own markers in any empty cell. The winner is the first person to get three of his or her own markers in a row, horizontally, vertically, or diagonally. There are six possible ways to win.

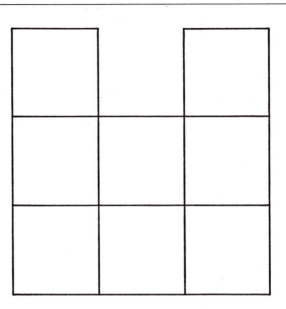

Figure A–2. Valley Tic-Tac-Toe Game Board

3. Mountain Tic-Tac-Toe

The game is played on a nine-cell board as shown in Figure A–3. Again, the rules of Tic-Tac-Toe are followed. The winner is the first person to get three of his or her markers in a row. There are seven ways to win.

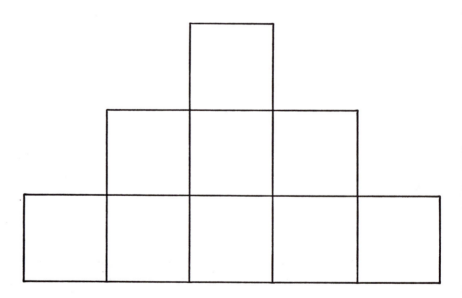

Figure A–3.　Mountain Tic-Tac-Toe Game Board

4. Reverse Tic-Tac-Toe

This game follows the rules of Tic-Tac-Toe described in game number 1. It simply changes the requirements for a win. Players must take turns placing an O or an X on the basic, nine-cell game board, and try to *avoid* getting three markers in a row. If a person gets three of his or her markers in a row, the opponent has won the game. Notice that the idea of Reverse Tic-Tac-Toe can be used with Valley and Mountain Tic-Tac-Toe as well.

5. Big 7 Tic-Tac-Toe

This game is played on a playing surface consisting of 49 squares in a 7 × 7 array. Two players take turns placing either an O or an X in any open cell on the playing surface. Each places his or her own mark. The first player to get four marks in a row is the winner.

6. Three-Person Tic-Tac-Toe

Most versions of Tic-Tac-Toe are games between two players. In this version, however, three people play. Players use either an X, an O, or an I as a marker, and the game is played on a board that contains a 6 × 6 or 36-cell array. Players put their own mark anywhere on the playing surface in turn. The first player to get three of his or her own markers in a row is the winner.

7. Line Tic-Tac-Toe

Fifteen dots are placed in a straight line. Two players alternate turns placing an X through any one dot anywhere on the line. The first player to mark off a dot so that there are three consecutive dots marked is the winner. The game can also be played as in Reverse Tic-Tac-Toe, so that the first player to mark the third consecutive X in the row is the *loser*.

8. Dots-in-a-Row Tic-Tac-Toe

The game is played on a surface as shown in Figure A-4. Players take turns crossing out as many dots as they desire, provided the dots are all along the same straight line. The player who crosses out the last dot is the winner.

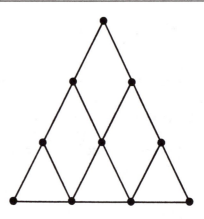

Figure A–4. Dots-in-a-Row Tic-Tac-Toe Game Board

9. Put 'Em Down Tic-Tac-Toe

Instead of making marks on a Tic-Tac-Toe board, each player is provided with three markers or other playing pieces. These are alternately placed on any of the line intersections (circles) on the playing surface in Figure A–5. The center circle may *not* be used by either player as his or her first play. After all the playing pieces have been placed, each player in turn moves one of his or her own pieces along a line to the next vacant circle. The winner is the first player to get three of his or her own pieces in a row, either vertically, horizontally, or diagonally.

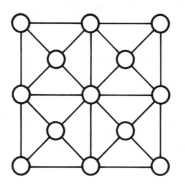

Figure A–5. Playing Board for Put 'Em Down Tic-Tac-Toe

10. Tac-Tic-Toe

This game is played on a 4 × 4 square surface. Each player has four chips or markers of a single color. The starting position is shown in Figure A–6(a). Players take turns moving a single piece of their own color. A move consists of moving one piece onto a vacant square either horizontally or vertically, but not diagonally. There is no jumping or capturing in this game. No piece can be moved into an already occupied square, but must be moved into an open, adjacent square. The winner is the player who moves three of his or her own pieces into a row, either horizontally, vertically, *or diagonally*, with no intervening spaces or intervening squares occupied by an opponent's pieces.

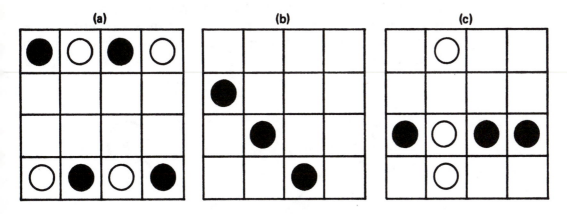

Figure A–6. (a) Starting Position for Tac-Tic-Toe; (b) Win Position for Tac-Tic-Toe; (c) Nobody Wins in These Positions

11. Triangular Tic-Tac-Toe

This game uses the basic rule—that is, the player placing three of his or her marks in a straight line is the winner. The playing surface, however, has been changed to the triangular array shown in Figure A–7, rather than the usual square array.

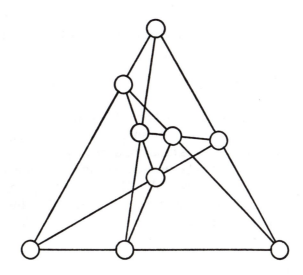

Figure A–7. Triangular Tic-Tac-Toe Board

BLOCKING STRATEGY GAMES

12. Blockade

Playing pieces are placed on cells A and B in Figure A–8 for player number one, and on cells C and D for player number two. Players take turns moving one playing piece along lines on the playing surface into any vacant, adjacent circle. No jumps or captures are permitted. A player loses the game when he or she cannot move either of his or her two pieces in his or her turn.

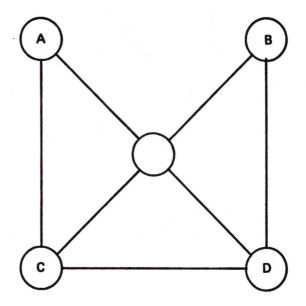

Figure A–8. Playing Surface for Blockade

13. Jest

This game is played on a 3 × 3 array of squares. Each player has three chips or markers of a single color. Starting position is as shown in Figure A–9. Players take turns moving one of their own pieces. Each piece may be moved one square in any direction: forward, backward, horizontally, or diagonally. There is no jumping of pieces, nor may a piece be captured. A player is a winner when his or her pieces occupy the opponent's starting line.

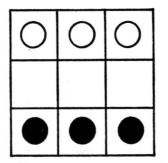

Figure A–9. Starting Position for Jest

14. Hex

The game of Hex is played on a diamond-shaped board made up of hexagons (see Figure A–10). The players take turns placing an X or an O in any hexagon on the board that is unoccupied. The winner is the first player to make an unbroken path from one side of the board to the other. Blocking moves and other strategies should be developed as the game proceeds. The corner hexagons belong to either player.

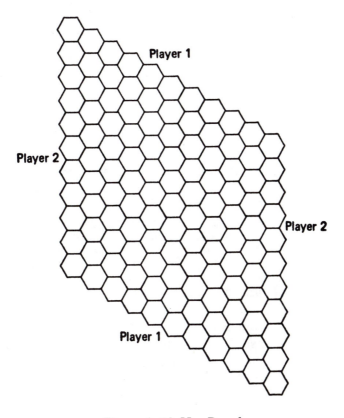

Figure A–10. Hex Board

15. The Four-Color Game

This game can be played by two, three, or four players. The game board is divided into various numbers of regions. One example is shown in Figure A–11. Each player, in turn, colors any region of his or her choice with an identifiable color. However, the regions adjacent to each other *may not* be of the same color. The first player who cannot make a move is the loser. Play continues until only one player is left. This player is the winner. Various colored chips or markers can be used instead of color pencils if you wish.

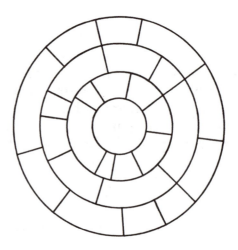

Figure A–11. A Game Board for the Four-Color Game

16. Bi-Squares

This game is played on a playing surface that consists of 16 squares in one continuous row. Players take turns placing their mark (an X for player number one, and an O for player number two) into each of two adjacent, unoccupied squares anywhere on the board. The player who makes the last successful move on the board is the winner.

17. Domino Cover

This game is played on the standard 8 × 8 square checkerboard, and uses a set of dominoes that will cover two adjacent squares, either horizontally or vertically. Players take turns placing a domino anywhere on the board, according to the following rules: (1) Player number one can only place his or her dominoes in a horizontal direction;

(2) player number two can only place dominoes in a vertical direction. The loser is the player who cannot make a move by placing a domino in the correct position.

18. Connecting Dots

The game is played on an 8 × 8 array of 64 dots as shown in Figure A–12. Players alternate turns to connect any two vertically or horizontally adjacent dots (but not diagonally) with a straight pencil line. The player who draws the line that completes a one-by-one unit square places his or her initial inside the square and goes again. When the board is completely covered with initials, the player with the most squares having his or her initial is the winner.

Figure A–12. A Game Board for Connecting Dots

19. Tromino Saturation

The game is played on a 5 × 5 square board. The playing pieces consist of the two basic tromino shapes shown in Figure A–13. Each tromino piece should exactly cover three squares on the playing board. Players alternate turns to place one of the pieces of either shape anywhere on the playing surface. The first player who cannot place a piece exactly covering three squares is the loser. (In order to allow each player a full choice of which piece to select on each play, prepare eight pieces of each shape.) If the size of the board is increased to a 6 × 6 board, prepare twelve pieces of each shape.

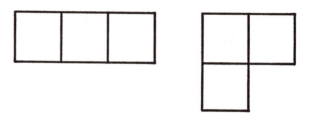

Figure A–13. The Two Basic Tromino Shapes for Saturation

CAPTURE STRATEGY GAMES

20. Short Checkers

This game is played on a 6 × 6 square checkerboard, rather than on the traditional 8 × 8 square board. Each player uses six checkers of his or her own color, and places them in the starting position on the black squares in the first two rows. The game is played according to the same rules as the traditional game of checkers, that uses twelve checkers for each player.

21. Solitaire

This is a strategy game for one person. In actuality, the player is competing against the board. The playing surface consists of a board with fifteen circles, as shown in Figure A–14. Place chips or other counters on all of the cells except the darkened cell. The players must remove as many counters as possible by jumping counters over adjacent counters (along lines) into empty cells. The jumped counters are removed from the board. All counters but one can be removed in this

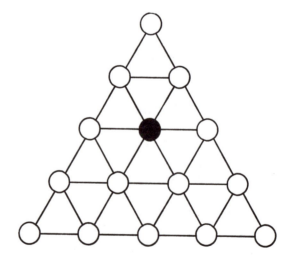

Figure A–14. Solitaire Board

manner. A winning game is one in which only one counter remains. A variation for experienced players is to try to make the one remaining counter end the game in the darkened cell.

22. Fox and Geese

This game for two players is played on a surface with 33 cells as shown in Figure A–15, The fox marker (with the black center) and the thirteen goose markers are shown in the figure. The fox can move in any direction along a line—up, down, left, or right. The geese move one cell at a time along the lines, but may not move backwards. The fox can capture a goose by making a short jump over a single goose along a line into the next cell, provided that the cell is vacant. The fox can make successive jumps on any one turn, provided vacant cells exist. The geese win if they can corner the fox so that he cannot move. The fox wins if he captures enough geese so they cannot corner him.

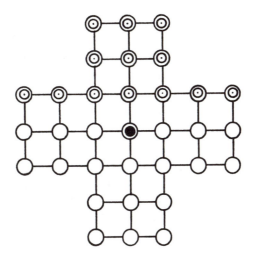

Figure A–15. Starting Position for Fox and Geese

23. Sprouts

Three dots are placed in a triangular array on a piece of paper. Players take turns drawing a line connecting any two dots, or connecting a dot to itself. After a line is drawn, a new dot is placed approximately midway between the two dots being connected, along the connecting line. No lines may cross, and no more than three lines may terminate in a single point. The last player to make a successful move is the winner. See Figure A–16. The new point, D, is shown along the line connecting point A to itself. The new point, E, is shown along the line connecting B to C. Notice that points D, E, and A each have two lines terminating.

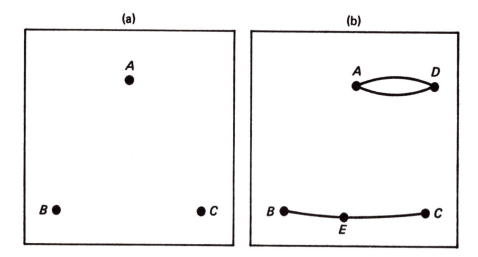

Figure A–16. (a) Sprouts Board; (b) Typical Moves in Sprouts

24. Nim

The game is played with a set of eleven chips, bottle caps, or other markers. The markers are placed on the table between the two players. In turn, each player may pick up one, two, or three chips. The winner is the player who picks up the last chip. Note: The game may also be played so that the person who picks up the final chip is the loser.

24. Sum 15

The game is played on a nine-cell, 3 x 3 square board. Player number one uses the five digits 1, 3, 5, 7, and 9. Player number two uses the five digits 2, 4, 6, 8, and 0. The players decide who will go first. The players alternate turns writing one of their own digits in any empty square on the board. Each digit may be used only once in a game. The winner is the player who completes a row of three numbers, either horizontally, vertically, or diagonally, with a sum of 15.

SOME COMMERCIAL STRATEGY GAMES

1. Amoeba

This is a game in which players rotate individual pieces on the game board as they attempt to form amoeba-like shapes that match the shapes on the cards in their hands. No two shapes are the same on the 54 cards in the deck. (Pressman Toys)

2. Basis

A strategy A game in which players form numerals in different bases while preventing their opponents from doing the same. (Holt, Rinehart and Winston Co.)

3. Battleship

A game of strategy in which two players try to sink each other's ships, which are hidden from view. It is a good introduction to coordinates. (Creative Publications)

4. Bee Line

Players use strategy while attempting to make a "beeline" across the playing board. (SEE Corporation)

5. Block 'N Score

A strategy game for two players who work in binary notation. (Creative Publications)

6. Equations

A game designed to give students practice in abstract reasoning, to increase speed and accuracy in computing, and to teach some of the basic concepts of mathematics. The game can be varied to work in different bases for more advanced students. (Wff'N Proof)

7. Foo (Fundamental Order of Operations)

A strategy game in which players try to combine seven cards into any multiple of twelve. Extra cards are drawn and discarded until one player calls "Foo!" (Cuisenaire, Inc.)

8. Helix

Another three-dimensional Tic-Tac-Toe game. Players place different-colored beads on a series of pins, trying to get four in a row. The pins are not only in straight lines, but also along arcs designated on the playing surface. (Creative Publications)

9. Kalah

A strategy game involving counting, skill, advanced planning, and logic. Chances is a minimal factor in this game. (Creative Publications)

10. Mastermind

A secret code of colored pegs is set up out of sight off one player. He or she then has ten chances to duplicate the colors and exact positions of the code pegs. Pure logic! (Cadaco, Invicta, Creative Publications)

11. Numble

A game similar to a crossword puzzle. Players place tiles with numerals from 0 to 9 on them to form addition, subtraction, multiplication, and division problems. (Math Media, Inc.)

12. Othello

A strategy game for two players that includes the moves and strategy of chess, checkers, and backgammon. Pieces change colors from player to player as the game progresses. (Gabriel Toys)

13. Pressups

A player must guide the direction of play so as to press down pegs of his or her own color. Traps must be set. The winner is the player who has more of his or her own color pegs depressed. (Invicta)

14. Qubic

Qubic expands Tic-Tac-Toe into a four-level space game. Players win by setting four markers in a straight line in one or several planes. (Parker Brothers)

15. Raco

By drawing from the pile, players attempt to replace cards in their racks so that the numbers read from high to low in numerical sequence. (Milton Bradley and Company)

16. Rubik's Brain Game

A game similar to Mastermind, but played with a Rubik's Cube. Players ask questions in order to determine the hidden 3×3 pattern of colors as they might appear on a Rubik's Cube. A game of logic and deduction. (Ideal Toys)

17. Score Four

Similar to Qubic and Helix. Players place wooden beads on metal pins and need to get four in a row to score. (Lakeside Toys)

18. *SOMA* Cube

An elegant cube with irregular sets of combinations of cubes. There are 1,105,920 mathematically different ways to come up with the 240 ways that the seven SOMA pieces fit together to form the original cube. (Parker Brothers)

19. Triominos

Triangular pieces replace the standard two–square dominoes in this game. Players must plan ahead to make matching numbers fit on all three sides of the piece that is being played. (Pressman Toys)

SECTION B

A Collection of
Non-Routine Problems

The following set of problems has been chosen to provide practice in reasoning and problem solving for your students. We have attempted to arrange the problems in increasing order of student maturity. However, the actual choice of problems for a particular student or group of students must be made by the classroom teacher. Only he or she is in a position to determine the appropriateness of a given problem for a particular child.

Notice, too, that the problems are all presented in written form. Obviously, many of the problems will have to be presented to the children orally, since the reading level may be beyond that of the students.

PROBLEM 1 Connect the numbers from 1 through 20, in order. (See Figure B–1.)

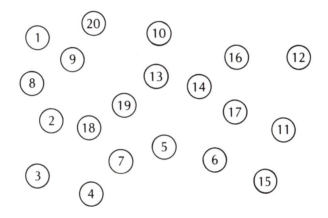

Figure B–1

Discussion While this problem may appear easy, it does require that younger children be able to count from 1 through 20 in order. As such, it is appropriate for younger children.

PROBLEM 2 Spot is 5 pounds heavier than Prince. Trixie is 3 pounds heavier than Spot. Spot weighs 35 pounds. How much does Trixie weigh?

Discussion The fact that Spot is 5 pounds heavier than Prince is not needed. The children should be made sensitive to the fact that some problems will contain extraneous information.

PROBLEM 3 When I stand on my stilts, my feet are as high as the top of my head when I am standing on the ground. The top of my head is 80 inches from the ground when I am standing on my stilts. How tall am I?

Discussion   Make a drawing (Figure B–2). Show, with arrows, the heights on the stilts as indicated. I am 40 inches tall.

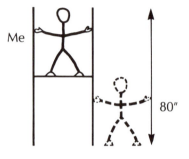

Figure B–2

PROBLEM 4   What's next?

(a)   1,   2,   3,   4,   _____
(b)   2,   4,   6,   _____

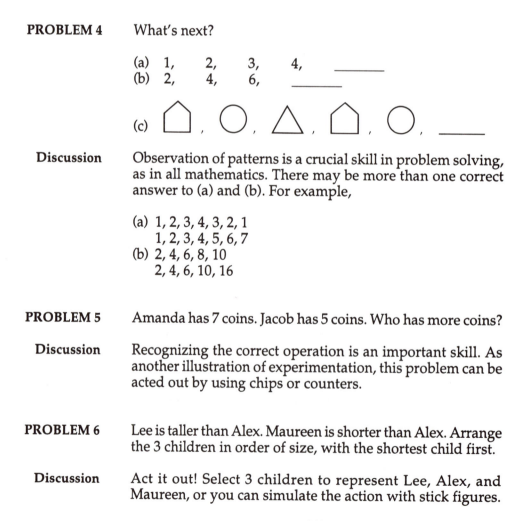

Discussion   Observation of patterns is a crucial skill in problem solving, as in all mathematics. There may be more than one correct answer to (a) and (b). For example,

(a) 1, 2, 3, 4, 3, 2, 1
     1, 2, 3, 4, 5, 6, 7
(b) 2, 4, 6, 8, 10
     2, 4, 6, 10, 16

PROBLEM 5   Amanda has 7 coins. Jacob has 5 coins. Who has more coins?

Discussion   Recognizing the correct operation is an important skill. As another illustration of experimentation, this problem can be acted out by using chips or counters.

PROBLEM 6   Lee is taller than Alex. Maureen is shorter than Alex. Arrange the 3 children in order of size, with the shortest child first.

Discussion   Act it out! Select 3 children to represent Lee, Alex, and Maureen, or you can simulate the action with stick figures.

140

PROBLEM 7   Andrea is taller than Michael. Danielle is taller than Michael. Arrange the 3 children in order of size, with the shortest child first.

Discussion   There is not enough information to solve this problem. We *can* decide that Michael is the shortest person, but we cannot arrange the other 2 in order. Students should be taught that, in some cases, a problem will not contain sufficient information to determine an answer.

PROBLEM 8   Amanda's grandfather gave her 6 nickels. She put them into her 3 piggy banks. How much did she put into each bank?

Discussion   Traditionally, this problem would have stated that she put the same number of coins in each bank. By not placing that restriction, we have opened up the problem to several answers. Since all the coins are the same, we need only focus on the number of coins in each bank. There could be 1-1-4, 1-2-3, or 2-2-2. Thus she put 5¢-5¢-20¢, or 5¢-10¢-15¢, or 10¢-10¢-10¢ in the banks.

PROBLEM 9   In our classroom, I have spelling before art. I have math right after art. Which class comes first?

Discussion   Have the students draw a time line. The answer requires a knowledge of the words "before" and "after" and their meanings.

PROBLEM 10   Bianca jumped from the 4-foot line and landed on the 9-foot line. Joanne jumped from the 2-foot line and landed on the 6-foot line. Who had the longer jump?

Discussion   Use a number line to determine the length of each jump, or depend on the students' understanding of subtraction and their knowledge of the basic subtraction facts.

PROBLEM 11   Jeff, Amy, and Tracy each have a different pet. One child has a bird, one has a cat, and the last child has a dog. Match each pet with its owner.

Amy's pet has 4 legs.
Jeff's pet doesn't bark.
Tracy is allergic to cats.
Jeff's pet does not fly.

Discussion   This is an example of a simple logic problem that can be solved by setting up a 3 × 3 matrix.

	Cat	Dog	Bird
Amy	X	Yes	X
Jeff	Yes	X	X
Tracy	X	X	Yes

Thus, Amy has the dog, Jeff has the cat, and Tracy has the bird.

PROBLEM 12   Nancy woke up at 8:00 A.M.
Danny woke up one hour after Nancy.
Jeff woke up two hours before Nancy.
At what time did Danny wake up ?

Discussion   This problem contains excess information. Careful reading is necessary. The question requires only the information about Nancy and Danny.

PROBLEM 13   David woke up at 7:00 A.M.
Barbara woke up one hour after David.
Suzie woke up two hours before Barbara.
At what time did Suzie wake up?

Discussion   Careful reading will reveal that *all* of the information in the problem is needed. David woke up at 7:00 A.M.; Barbara woke up one hour later—8:00 A.M. Suzie woke up two hours before Barbara—6:00 A.M.

PROBLEM 14   How many triangles whose vertices total 15 can you draw on the map in Figure B–3 ?

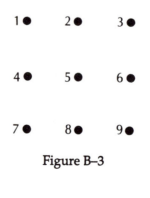

Figure B–3

Discussion

Any three points whose sum is 15 will satisfy the given conditions, as long as the points are *not* colinear. For example, 2 + 5 + 8 will give a sum of 15, but will not form a triangle. Similarly, the 2 diagonals. There are 4 triangles that answer the given problem: 1-6-8; 2-4-9; 2-6-7; 3-4-8.

PROBLEM 15

The teacher collected notebooks from each student in the class and piled them up on her desk. There are 12 notebooks above yours and 14 notebooks below yours. How many notebooks does the teacher have on her desk?

Discussion

The key to this problem is the fact that there is a dividing notebook between the 12 above and the 14 below. Thus, there are 27 notebooks in all. Some students may have to use manipulatives to see this.

PROBLEM 16

The circus train has 40 cars. The elephants are in the twelfth car and the clowns are in the twenty-second car. How many cars are between the elephants and the clowns?

Discussion

The 40 cars in the circus train is extra information (a distractor). Have the children use manipulatives to simulate the situation. There are 9 cars *between* the elephants and the clowns.

PROBLEM 17

The Bulldogs scored 35 points. The Pumas scored 9 points more. How many points did the Pumas score?

Discussion

This problem depends on the students' understanding the concept of "more" as being addition.

PROBLEM 18

Tom scored Tic-Tac-Toe, Three in a Row! When he added the three numbers under his X's, he got a sum of 30. On what numbers did Tom's three X's fall?

8	12	14
6	10	5
9	13	11

Discussion

Here is an opportunity for students to use a calculator to solve the problem. Have them add the sums in all the columns, rows and diagonals: 14 + 5 + 11 = 30

PROBLEM 19   How many ways can you get from A to B in Figure B–4 ?

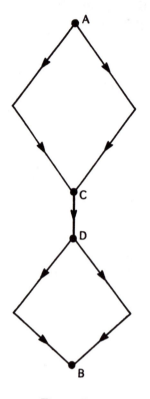

Figure B–4

Discussion   There are 2 ways to go from A to C and 2 ways to go from D to B. Thus there are 2 × 2 or 4 ways to go from A to B. This is the fundamental counting principle; however, most students should actually trace the paths.

PROBLEM 20   Mula bought a set of wind chimes for his backyard. The set has 4 different geometric shapes. The square is between the circle and the triangle. The rectangle is on the bottom. The circle is on the top. From top to bottom, in what order are the shapes?

Discussion   Have the students draw a vertical line. The circle is on the top and the rectangle is on the bottom. Since the square is between the circle and the triangle, the order from top to bottom is circle, square, triangle, rectangle.

PROBLEM 21   Harriet has 5 books. Libby has 12 books. Mark has more books than Harriet, but fewer books than Libby. How many books might Mark have?

Discussion   The answer is any number from 6 through 11. However, if we alter the problem by removing the condition that Mark has fewer books than Libby, then the number of books that Mark might have is open-ended. This is a good concept for younger children to consider.

PROBLEM 22   What are the colors of the last 2 beads in Figure B–5?

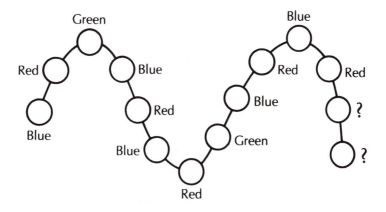

Figure B–5

Discussion   Look for a pattern. One possible pattern would be to group the beads in groups of 5: blue-red-green-blue-red. Thus, the last 2 beads would be green-blue.

PROBLEM 23   Daniel, Michael, and Jeffrey made 13 baskets to be sold at the school crafts fair. Each boy made a different number of baskets, and no one made more than 6. Daniel made twice as many baskets as Michael. How many baskets did each boy make?

Discussion   Guess and test with an organized list. We obtain two possible sets of answers, 2-5-6 and 3-4-6. However, since Daniel made twice as many baskets as Michael, only the 3-4-6 set will satisfy the conditions of the problem. Thus, Daniel made 6 baskets, Jeffrey made 4 baskets, and Michael made 3 baskets.

PROBLEM 24 In Figure B–6, how would you get exactly 2 pints of water?

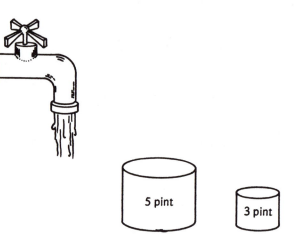

Figure B–6

Discussion This problem provides the child with an early experience in guess and test as well as in logic. The procedure would be to fill the 5-pint bucket with water and pour it into the 3-pint bucket. There will be the required 2 pints of water remaining in the 5-pint bucket.

PROBLEM 25 Using the same drawing as in Figure B–6, how would you obtain exactly 1 pint?

Discussion This problem is another example of the guess and test strategy together with logic. The procedure would be to fill the 3-pint bucket and pour the water into the 5-pint bucket. Now refill the 3-pint bucket and pour just enough of this water into the 5-pint bucket to fill it. This will leave exactly 1 pint in the 3-pint bucket.

PROBLEM 26 James has 3 banks. One is shaped like an elephant, one is shaped like a giraffe, and one is shaped like a turtle. Each bank has some nickels in it. There is 45¢ in all. We know the following facts:

1. The elephant bank is not empty.

2. The elephant bank has less in it than the giraffe bank.
3. The elephant bank has less in it than the turtle bank.
4. The turtle bank has less in it than the giraffe bank.

How much money is in each bank?

Discussion   This problem can be done with pencil and paper, or it may be one by acting out the conditions with chips. Actually, this may be the first time some of the children are confronted by a problem having more than one correct answer. There are three:

> elephant 5¢—turtle 10¢—giraffe 30¢
> elephant 5¢—turtle 15¢—giraffe 25¢
> elephant 10¢—turtle 15¢—giraffe 20¢

PROBLEM 27   In Figure B–7, each box has the same number of pencils inside. How many pencils are in each box?

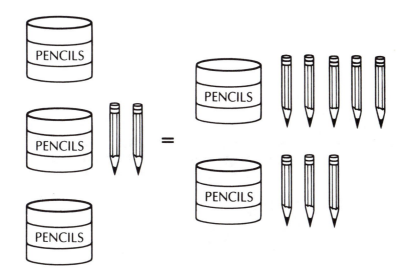

Figure B–7

Discussion   This is an opportunity to introduce the properties of equality through the use of manipulatives.
Step 1: Remove 2 boxes of pencils from each side. This leaves 1 box and 2 pencils on the left, and 8 pencils on the right.
Step 2: Remove 2 pencils from each side. This leaves 1 box on the left and 6 pencils on the right.
Thus, 1 box contains 6 pencils.

PROBLEM 28

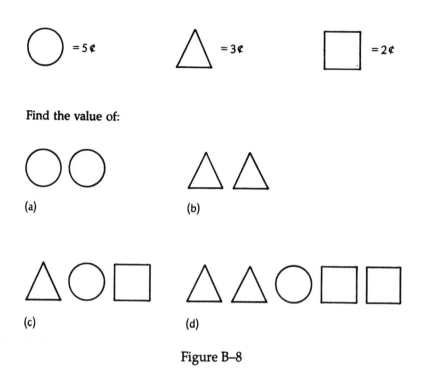

Find the value of:

Figure B–8

Discussion   Symbolizing numerical values with geometric figures is analogous to algebraic representation. The answers are obtained by replacing each symbol with its given value. Thus,

(a) 5¢ + 5¢ = 10¢
(b) 3¢ + 3¢ = 6¢
(c) 3¢ + 5¢ + 2¢ = 10¢
(d) 3¢ + 3¢ + 5¢ + 2¢ + 2¢ = 15¢

PROBLEM 29

Make a picture worth 20¢.

Discussion　Just as in the previous problem, symbolic representation is carefully stressed. However, this problem requires a higher level of creativity, since it is more open-ended. Answers will vary. For example, see Figure B–9.

20¢ =

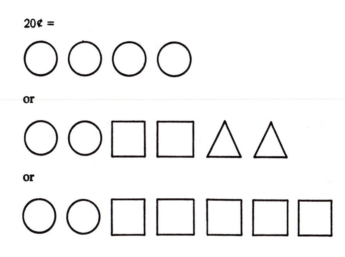

Figure B–9

PROBLEM 30　In Figure B–10, there is more than 1 coin in each of the 3 banks.
Banks A and B contain the same number of coins.
Bank C has the most coins.
If you multiply the number of coins in each bank together, the answer is 36.
How many coins are in each bank?

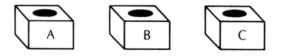

Figure B–10

Discussion　The picture and the first statement tell us that there are at least 2 coins in each of the 3 banks. The second clue tells us that there is the same number of coins in 2 banks. We are looking for 3 numbers whose product is 36; 2 of the numbers are the same. Thus there are two possible answers, namely 2-2-9 and 3-3-4. (Since the order is not important, 9–2–2 is the same as 2–2–9, etc.) Notice that the fact that bank C has the most coins is not needed. Children should be made aware of extraneous information as well as the multiple answers.

PROBLEM 31   Glenda made a stack of cubes alongside her desk. She discovered that the stack contained an even number of cubes. Then she made 2 more stacks of the cubes, each with the same number of cubes as her original stack. Was the total number of cubes in the stacks odd or even?

Discussion   Some students may actually wish to take a number of small cubes or chips and act out the problem. Others may simulate the action with a pencil and paper. In any case, the problem leads youngsters to see that the sum of 3 even numbers is even. Or, the product of 3 times an even number is even.

PROBLEM 32   Jim, Kim, and Lim had a race. Kim came in last. Lim did not win. Who won the race?

Discussion   The construction of a time line along with logical thinking reveals the placement of the 3 contestants: Kim was third, Lim was second, and Jim won the race.

PROBLEM 33   You can buy 1 marble for 1¢. Each additional marble costs 2¢. How much will you pay for 6 marbles? Finish the table.

Number of Marbles	1	2	3	4	5	6
Cost	1¢	3¢	5¢	7¢		

Discussion   Students must not only be able to read a table, but should also be able to complete a table that has already been started. As the number of marbles increases by 1, the cost increases by 2¢. Some children might be able to generalize the situation—the cost of the marbles is twice the number of marbles minus 1.

PROBLEM 34   Two of the patterns shown in Figure B–11 will fold up to form a cube. Which ones are they?

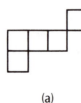
(a)

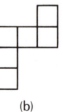
(b)

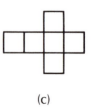
(c)

Figure B–11

Discussion   Notice that pattern (a) only contains 5 squares. Since a cube has 6 faces, only (b) and (c) can be folded to form a cube. Have the students make enlarged versions of (b) and (c) and then fold them to form a cube.

PROBLEM 35   July 4 is a Tuesday. Your birthday is on July 23. On what day of the week is your birthday?

Discussion   A good way of attacking this problem is to sketch a calendar for the month of July. The answer is easily found this way. An alternative method without drawing the calendar is to use the fact that a week contains 7 days. Thus July 11, 18, and 25 are also Tuesdays. Counting back from July 25 to July 23 places your birthday on a Sunday.

PROBLEM 36   In Figure B–12, move only 1 block to another stack so that the sum of the numbers in each stack is 12.

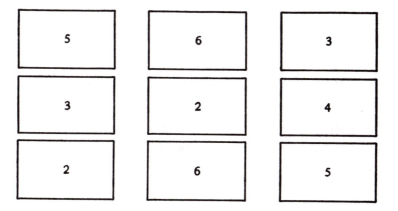

Figure B–12

Discussion   Some students will solve this problem by observation. Others will add the numerals in each stack. Help them to solve the problem by an experiment. Provide a set of 9 cubes with the numbers written on them. Have students stack them as shown and then actually shift them around. Or provide a set of buttons, tokens, or sticks and have the children actually do the problem.

PROBLEM 37   The new rock band, the Jumpin' Jeebies, is going to play in a school concert next Saturday night. The 4 members of the band are Jason, Jasmine, Jerome, and Jenine. Jerome and Jason have ears. Jerome does not have a nose. Jasmine and Jenine have hair. Jasmine has 5 blue spikes sticking out of the top of her head. What name goes with each picture in Figure B–13?

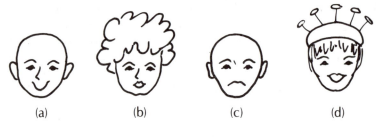

(a)   (b)   (c)   (d)

Figure B–13

Discussion   The students should take each clue in order, examining how the clue affects the pictures. The first clue, Jerome and Jason have ears, makes (a) and (c) the 2 boys. The fact that Jerome does not have a nose makes (c) Jerome and thus (a) is Jason. Similarly, we find that (b) is Jenine and (d) is Jasmine.

PROBLEM 38   1 put my 10 checkers into 2 piles. One pile has 4 more checkers than the other has. How many checkers are in each stack?

Discussion   Act it out! Give each student 10 checkers or buttons. Have them guess at the size of each pile and test their guess with the checkers. They should find that there are 7 checkers in 1 stack and 3 checkers in the other.

PROBLEM 39   In Figure B–14, how much time is left on the parking meter?

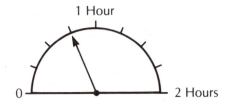

Figure B–14

Discussion

The drawing shows each hour divided into 4 sections, representing 15 minutes each. Thus the time used up is 1 hour and 15 minutes. If we subtract from 2 hours, we obtain 45 minutes. We could also count the number of sections left, namely 3, at 15 minutes each.

PROBLEM 40

There are 48 children in 2 clubs.
There are 15 boys in 1 of the clubs.
There are 10 boys in the other club.
How many girls are there in both clubs?

Discussion

Careful reading is especially necessary to solve this problem. All the information is given in terms of the number of boys. Students must add 15 + 10 = 25 (the total number of boys who are in the two clubs), and then subtract from 48 to get the total number of girls, 23.

PROBLEM 41

Tasha has a set of five weights: 5 ounces, 6 ounces, 8 ounces, 9 ounces, and 16 ounces. She wants to put them on a balance scale, so that the scale will balance. How can she distribute the five weights on the two pans so that the scale will balance?

Discussion

Since the scale will balance with 22 ounces on each side (the total weight of the five weights is 44 ounces), guess and test will reveal that Tasha must put the 16-ounce and the 6-ounce weights on one side, and the other three weights on the other side.

PROBLEM 42

How much less does it cost a family of 2 adults and 3 children to visit the aquarium on a weekday than on a Saturday?

**GRAND AQUARIUM OPENING!!!
SPECIAL PRICES**

<u>Monday–Friday</u>
Adults $4.50
Children $2.25

<u>Saturday and Sunday</u>
Adults $6.00
Children $3.00

Discussion   This problem is an example of a multi-stage problem. It should be carefully worked in separate parts.

Part 1: During the week

$$2 \times 4.50 = 9.00$$
$$3 \times 2.25 = 6.75$$
$$\overline{ \$15.75}$$

Part 2: Saturday

$$2 \times 6.00 = 12.00$$
$$3 \times 3.00 = 9.00$$
$$\overline{ \$21.00}$$

Part 3:

$$\$21.00$$
$$-15.75$$
$$\overline{\$5.25}$$

It would cost them $5.25 more to visit the aquarium on Saturday.

PROBLEM 43   How many rectangles do you see in Figure B–15?

Figure B–15

Discussion   There are four different sizes of rectangles in the figure: those composed of 1 small rectangle, those composed of 2 small rectangles, those composed of 3 small rectangles, and that composed of 4 rectangles. There are $4 + 3 + 2 + 1 = 10$ rectangles of all sizes.

PROBLEM 44   Last week, the Giants played the Dodgers. There were a total of 7 runs scored in the game. What could have been the final score?

154

Discussion   Make a list. There are 8 possible scores:

Giants	Dodgers
7	0
6	1
5	2
4	3
3	4
2	5
1	6
0	7

PROBLEM 45   Elton brought a pizza to school, cut into equal-size pieces. He ate half of the slices and gave the rest to his three friends. Each of his friends received 2 slices. How many slices was the pizza cut into?

Discussion   This problem can be simulated with paper and pencil or by using bottle caps or chips. Since 3 friends each received 2 slices, half of the pizza would be 6 slices. Thus the entire pizza had been cut into 12 slices.

PROBLEM 46   I have nine bills in my wallet. Five of them are $1 bills and the rest of them are $5 bills. How much money do I have in my wallet?

Discussion   This problem is a multi-step problem and should be done one part at a time.
Step 1: 9 bills − 5 $1 bills = 4 bills
Step 2: 4 bills × $5 each   = $20
Step 3: $20 + $5 = $25

PROBLEM 47   A chicken can lay about 5 eggs each week. How many eggs can you expect 5 chickens to lay in 3 weeks?

Discussion   Organize the work with a table:

1 chicken   = 5 eggs in 1 week
5 chickens = 25 eggs in 1 week
5 chickens = 75 eggs in 3 weeks

You can expect 75 eggs from 5 chickens in 3 weeks.

PROBLEM 48   Mrs. O'Brien has 3 children. Arlene is younger than Bonnie. Arlene is younger than Celeste. Bonnie is older than Celeste. The ages of the children are 6, 9, and 11. How old is Celeste?

Discussion   The first two facts establish Arlene as the youngest. The third fact establishes Bonnie as the oldest. Thus their ages are Arlene—6, Celeste—9, Bonnie—11.

PROBLEM 49   My school is $\frac{1}{2}$ mile from my house. How many miles do I walk if I walk to school in the morning, walk home for lunch, and then walk home after school?

Discussion   Either by making a drawing or talking about the action, the children should know that there are 4 one-way trips of $\frac{1}{2}$ mile each.

PROBLEM 50   You want to buy each of the 3 stamps in order to mail the letters shown in Figure B–16. You have the coins that are shown in the figure. Which coins would you use to buy each stamp? You will use all of your coins.

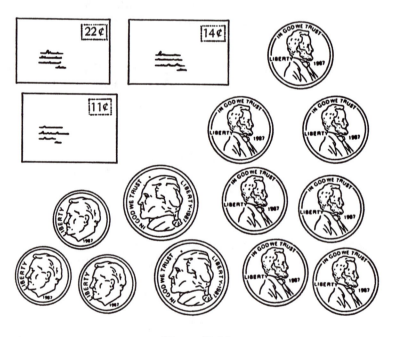

Figure B–16

Discussion   Let's simulate the action. Provide the students with coins or cutouts of coins. Allow them to guess and test until they arrive at the correct answer. The 22¢ stamp will be bought with 2 dimes and 2 pennies. The 14¢ stamp can be bought with 1 dime and 4 pennies. The ll¢ stamp is then bought, with the 2 nickels and 1 penny.

PROBLEM 51

Maureen has $9. Beth has $5. Penny has $6. Lois has $4. Two of the girls put their money together and had a total of $9. Who were the two girls?

Discussion

Guess and test! Have the students choose any 2 girls and find their total money. Continue until they guess Beth and Lois. $5 + $4 = $9. Notice that Maureen already has $9 by herself. Thus, she need not be counted in the problem since it calls for *two* girls with a total of $9.

PROBLEM 52

Which of the four numbers in the array doesn't belong? Why?

23	20
25	15

Discussion

This problem is very open-ended. Some students will decide that 23 doesn't belong, since it is the only number that does not contain 5 as a factor. Other students may decide that 15 doesn't belong, since it is the only number that does not have a ten's digit of 2. Others may eliminate 20, since it is the only even number in the array. All are correct!

PROBLEM 53

Jeff has 7 more baseball cards than Scott. Scott has 4 more baseball cards than Rick. Rick has 11 baseball cards. How many baseball cards does Jeff have?

Discussion

Work backwards. Rick has 11 baseball cards and Scott has 4 more than Rick; Scott has 15. Jeff has 7 more cards than Scott, so he has 22 baseball cards.

PROBLEM 54

A Boy Scout was walking south in the woods. He made a left turn and walked a little bit farther. Then he made another left turn and walked again. He made another left turn and walked, then he made one more left turn. In which direction is he now walking?

Discussion

Simulate the action in this problem with a drawing. Notice that when you make 4 left turns, you are walking in the same direction in which you started.

PROBLEM 55   In a line, there is a rabbit in front of 2 rabbits. There is a rabbit behind 2 rabbits. There is a rabbit between 2 rabbits. What is the smallest number of rabbits that could be in the line?

Discussion   Simulate the situation by drawing a series of lines similar to the following:

← ⊕ ⊢ ⊢ —	1 rabbit in front of 2 rabbits
← ⊢ ⊢ ⊕ —	1 rabbit behind 2 rabbits
← ⊢ ⊕ ⊢ —	1 rabbit between 2 rabbits

The answer to the problem is 3 rabbits. Notice that the problem called for the *smallest* number of rabbits in the line.

PROBLEM 56   Ann, Brad, Carol, and Daniel each wrote a report about a different kind of whale. Their reports were about blue whales, fin whales, humpbacks, and bowheads. Carol and Daniel did not write about humpbacks. Brad wrote about fin whales. Ann did not write about blue whales, and Daniel did not write about bowheads. Who wrote each report?

Discussion   Prepare a 4 × 4 matrix as shown. Use the clues to mark X when someone did not write about a certain kind of whale.

	Blue	Fin	Humpback	Bowhead
Ann	X	X	Yes	X
Brad	X	Yes	X	X
Carol	X	X	X	Yes
Daniel	Yes	X	X	X

The clues help us eliminate incorrect choices. Ann wrote about humpback whales, Brad wrote about fin whales, Carol wrote about bowhead whales, and Daniel wrote about blue whales.

PROBLEM 57   See Figure B–17. How far is the city from the state park? If you are halfway between the city and the state park, how far are you from the sign?

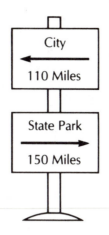

Figure B–17

Discussion   Make a line drawing. This shows 110 + 150 = 260. The city and the state park are 260 miles apart. When you are half-way between the city and the state park, you are 130 miles from each. Thus, you are 20 miles from the sign.

PROBLEM 58   In Figure B–18, which box would you take off the scale to make it balance?

Figure B–18

Discussion	In this problem, the fact must be obtained from an examination of the picture. This is a technique that students must practice. The problem employs the guess and test strategy. Remove 1 box at a time from the lower (heavier) side of the scale. Add the remaining numbers to see if both sides balance. Removing the 36 will make the boxes on each side total 161. Some students may find the sum of the boxes on each side (161 and 197 respectively), and then find the difference, 36.
PROBLEM 59	When Howard came to the bike rack, every slot was filled with a bike except the middle one, where he parked his bike. There were 8 bikes to the right of Howard's bike. How many bicycles are there in the rack?
Discussion	Make a drawing. Show Howard's bike in the center and show 8 bikes to the right of his bike. But, if Howard's bike is in the *middle*, there are also 8 bikes to the left of his bike. Thus, there are 8 + 8 + 1 (Howard's bike counts, too) for a total of 17 bikes in the rack. An alternate procedure using logic tells us that, if Howard's bike is in the middle, there will be just as many bikes on either side. Thus the 8 bikes on the right side equals the 8 bikes on the left side. Don't forget to count Howard's bike, too.
PROBLEM 60	Linda's class was planting saplings on Arbor Day. Linda planted a tree that is just 2 years old. She is 7 years old. How old will the tree be when Linda is 13 years old?
Discussion	Some students may recognize that Linda will *always* be 5 years older than the tree. Thus, the tree will be 8 years old when Linda is 13. Other students may wish to make a table to reveal the answer:

Linda's Age	7	8	9	. . .	13
Tree's Age	2	3	4	. . .	8

PROBLEM 61	Sonja's guppies had baby fish last week. She gave 6 of them to Beth and 5 of them to Nancy. If there were 18 baby fish to start, how many does Sonja keep?
Discussion	This is a multi-stage problem. Add the number of fish given away (6 + 5 = 11) and subtract this sum from the total number of fish to find the answer (18 - 11 = 7). Sonja kept 7 fish.

PROBLEM 62   Nancy and Ellen each start reading a copy of *Gone with the Wind* on the first day of their summer vacation. Nancy decides to read 7 pages each day, but Ellen only wants to read 5 pages each day. When Nancy is on page 84, what page is Ellen reading?

Discussion   One approach is to make a table such as the following:

Day	Nancy	Ellen
1	7	5
2	14	10
3	21	15
4	28	20
.	.	.
.	.	.
.	.	.
12	84	60

This problem can also be solved by the use of ratio and proportion:

$$\frac{7}{5} = \frac{84}{x}$$

Ellen will be reading page 60.

PROBLEM 63   The faces of a cube are numbered with consecutive numbers. Three faces of the cube are shown in Figure B–19. Find the sum of the numbers on the faces of the cube.

Figure B–19

Discussion   There are 6 faces on a cube. Since the numbers on the faces are consecutive, there are two possible answers:

$$25 + 26 + 27 + 28 + 29 + 30 = 165$$
$$26 + 27 + 28 + 29 + 30 + 31 = 171$$

Both answers are correct.

PROBLEM 64   Peter, Paul, and Mary have 5 cookies. How many ways can they divide the cookies if each person must get at least 1 cookie and they do not break any of the cookies?

Discussion   Make a table.

Peter	Paul	Mary
1	3	1
1	2	2
1	1	3
2	1	2
2	2	1
3	1	1

There are 6 different ways it can be done.

PROBLEM 65   How many 5¢ pieces of bubble gum can you buy if you have 33 pennies?

Discussion   Have your students act it out. Give them 33 counters and have them arrange them in sets of 5. Each set buys one piece of bubble gum. The remainder of 3 is not enough to buy another piece of gum. An alternate solution is to make a table:

Number of Pieces of Bubble Gum	1	2	3	4	5	6
Cost	5¢	10¢	15¢	20¢	25¢	30¢

The more mathematically mature student may divide 33 by 5 and disregard the remainder (which would not yield a fractional piece of bubble gum, as stores are unwilling to subdivide bubble gum pieces).

PROBLEM 66   The record store has a sale on cassette tapes at $4, $5, $6 and $7 each. Lorraine bought some tapes and paid $12. What were the prices of the tapes Lorraine bought?

Discussion   This problem is solved by guess and test. However, there is more than one correct answer. For example, she might have bought 1 tape for $7 and 1 tape for $5. Or she could have bought 2 tapes for $6 each. Or possibly 3 tapes at $4 each. It is important for students to meet problems with more than one correct answer.

PROBLEM 67 After finishing her shopping, Michelle came home with $3.00. She had spent $3.25 on a present for her sister Beth, $4.25 for balloons for the party, and $5.00 for invitations. How much did Michelle start with?

Discussion Students should work backwards to solve the problem:

$$
\begin{array}{rl}
\$ \ 3.00 & \text{Money she had left at the end} \\
+ \quad 5.00 & \text{Spent on invitations} \\
\hline
8.00 & \\
+ \quad 4.25 & \text{Spent on balloons} \\
\hline
12.25 & \\
+ \quad 3.25 & \text{Spent on a present} \\
\hline
\$ \ 15.50 & \text{Amount she started with}
\end{array}
$$

Have the students check their work by beginning with the $15.50 and carrying the action forward. Do they finish with $3.00, as the problem stated?

PROBLEM 68 The houses on my street all have odd numbers. The first house is number 3, the second house is number 5. The third house is number 7, and so on. What is the number of the tenth house?

Discussion A table reveals the answer. Follow the pattern in each row of the list.

House	1	2	3	4	5	6	7	8	9	10
Number	3	5	7	9	11	13	15	17	19	21

The tenth house is number 21. Some students may notice the generalization that can be seen in the table—namely, multiply the location of the house by 2 and add 1 to the product $(2 \times h + 1)$.

PROBLEM 69 What's next in each of these sequences?

(a) 23, 29, 35, 41, ____, ____.
(b)   1,   1,   2,   3, 5, 8, 13,   ____, ____.
(c)   3, 12,   5,   9, 7, 6, 9,   ____, ____.

(d)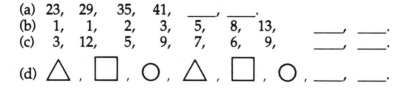

Discussion   Students should *describe orally* the pattern rule for each series. In (a), each term is increased by 6. The missing terms are 47 and 53. In (b) the sequence is the well-known Fibonacci sequence where each term after the first two is found by adding the two previous terms. The next two terms would thus be 21 and 34. In (c), the students must realize that there are really two embedded sequences. The odd-numbered terms are increasing by 2 (3, 5, 7, 9) while the even-numbered terms are decreasing by 3 (12, 9, 6). The missing terms are 3 and 11. In (d) the sequence of shapes repeats after every three terms. The next two terms would be the triangle and the square.

PROBLEM 70   There is a boy in front of 2 girls and a boy behind 2 girls. There is a boy between 2 girls. What is the smallest number of children that could be in the line?

Discussion   Have the students simulate the action with a drawing or with manipulatives. They may also decide to act out the problem. There are 5 children in line; the arrangement would be girl-girl-boy-girl-girl.

PROBLEM 71   Helen works in a pet store. One of her jobs is to clean the canary cage each morning. Last Tuesday when she opened the door, the canaries flew out and half of them flew right out of the store. Of the ones that were left, 2 flew out of the cage and landed on the parrot cage, 5 landed on the tank that holds the goldfish, and the remaining 8 flew into the room where the birdseed is stored. How many canaries were in the cage when Helen opened the door?

Discussion   Work backwards.

$$
\begin{array}{rl}
8 = & \text{The number in the birdseed room} \\
+ \ 5 = & \text{The number on the goldfish tank} \\
+ \ 2 = & \text{The number on the parrot cage} \\
\hline
15 = & \text{One-half the total number} \\
30 = & \text{The number that were in the cage originally}
\end{array}
$$

PROBLEM 72   Irv has 6 baseball cards. Bob has 4 baseball cards. Steve has 3 baseball cards. Sandra has 7 baseball cards, and Marcella has 9 baseball cards. Three of them put their cards together and had a total of 18 cards. Who put their cards together?

Discussion   Guess and test. Try different combinations of 3 people until we get 18 cards. The answer is Irv (6), Steve (3), and Marcella (9).

PROBLEM 73   Some children took 5 rides in a pony cart. Only 1 child went on the first ride, 3 children went on the second ride, and 5 children went on the third ride. Louis guessed that 9 children went on the fifth ride. Can you tell why Louis made that guess?

Discussion   The children should realize that Louis found a pattern. The pattern yields the sequence 1, 3, 5, <u>7</u>, <u>9</u>.

PROBLEM 74   Arlene bought 3 different toys for her children. The gifts cost her $24. What did she buy?

Pop-up Book	$5	Roller Skates	$12
Game	$7	Baseball Glove	$9
Model Cars	$6		

Discussion   Use guess and test. The answer is a pop-up book, roller skates, and a game.

PROBLEM 75   Andrew is making his lunch for school. He makes sandwiches with either white bread or rye bread. He can use cheese or jelly or lunch meat. How many different sandwiches can he make?

Discussion   Make a list of all possible sandwiches:

White Bread	Rye Bread
cheese	cheese
jelly	jelly
meat	meat

He can make 6 different sandwiches. Some students may argue that the sandwich could be made with 1 slice of rye bread and 1 slice of white bread. These students will have 3 additional sandwiches, for a total of 9.

PROBLEM 76   Rhoda, Sal, and Terry were scheduled to meet at the Town Hall at a certain time. The times at which they actually arrived were 11:05, 11:20, and 11:30. Rhoda arrived 5 minutes late. Sal arrived 10 minutes early, and Terry arrived 15 minutes late. At what time were they supposed to meet? At what time did each person arrive?

Discussion   Use logic. Since Sal was the only one to arrive early, and since 11:05 was the earliest arrival time, Sal was the one who arrived first (because the other 2 were both late). He was ten minutes early, thus the scheduled meeting time must have been 11:15. Rhoda arrived at 11:20 (5 minutes late) and Terry arrived at 11:30 (15 minutes late).

PROBLEM 77   Jan and Marissa both swim at the local pool for exercise. They met each other while swimming on July 2. Marissa asked, "How often do you swim?" "I swim every third day, so my next workout will be on July 5," said Jan. "Well, I swim every fourth day, so my next workout will be on July 6," said Marissa. On what dates in July will the 2 girls both swim if they stick to their schedules?

Discussion   Make a table of the dates on which each of the girls will swim:

Jan	2	5	8	11	14	17	20	23	26	29
Marissa	2	6	10	14	18	22	26	30		

Both girls will swim on July 2, 14, and 26. A more elegant solution can be obtained by recognizing that 3 and 4 are relatively prime and their least common multiple is 12. Thus, 2 + 12 = 14, 14 + 12 = 26.

PROBLEM 78   Carl went running up to his teacher, all excited. "Look what I just discovered," he said. "When I open my math book to any page and add the page numbers of the 2 facing pages, I always get an odd number, but when I multiply them, I always get an even number." Is Carl right? If so, can you explain why it happens?

Discussion   Facing pages of a book are always consecutive whole numbers. Thus one is always an odd number and 1 is always an even number. The sum of an odd and an even number is always odd; the product of an odd and an even number will always be even.

PROBLEM 79   Rulak is gathering up his friends to play a game of interplanetary hockey. His friends live in his galaxy, but on different planets. Rulak flies 4 planets west to get his friend, Reek. Reek lives on the first planet in the galaxy. Then Rulak flies east 8 planets to get Rook. From there, he flies west 7 planets to get Rork. He then flies east 10 planets for Rak, who

166

lives on the last planet in the galaxy. How many planets are there in Rulak's galaxy?

Discussion   Draw a number line. Pick one point on the line for Rulak's planet. Follow the directions. The results will be as shown:

1	2	5	9	12
Reek	Rork	Rulak	Rook	Rak

PROBLEM 80   Theresa is older than Steve. Steve is younger than Maurice. Maurice is younger than Theresa. Ben is older than Theresa. Their ages are 10, 12, 14, and 16. How old is Maurice?

Discussion   The facts in this problem can be arranged on a timeline. This will reveal the ages of the children as Steve—10, Maurice—12, Theresa—14, and Ben—16.

PROBLEM 81   It is possible to make each of the amounts of money listed in the diagram by using exactly 6 coins. Record your answers on the given table.

Amount	1¢	5¢	10¢	25¢	50¢
.42					
.85					
$1.26					
$1.70					

Discussion   This is a problem that can be solved by using manipulatives and guess and test. There may be multiple answers for each amount. One possible set of answers is shown:

Amount	1¢	5¢	10¢	25¢	50¢
.42	2	0	4	0	0
.85	0	1	3	2	0
$1.26	1	0	0	5	0
$1.70	0	2	1	0	3

PROBLEM 82   A bus with 53 people on it makes 2 stops. At the first stop, 17 people get off and 19 people get on. At the second stop, 28 people get off and 23 get on. How many people are now on the bus?

Discussion   This problem requires careful reading and careful record keeping. Make a table.

Stop#	People Off	People On	On Board
—	—	—	53
1	53 – 17 = 36	36 + 19 =	55
2	55 – 28 = 27	27 + 23 =	50

There are now 50 people on board the bus.

PROBLEM 83   You are waiting for the elevator to take you to the observation tower on the seventieth floor of the Hancock Building. There are 45 people in line ahead of you. If each elevator can carry 10 people, on which trip will you be ?

Discussion   The fact that the observation tower is on the seventieth floor is excess information. If 10 people go on each trip, the first 4 trips of the elevator will take 40 people. You will be on the fifth trip. Some children may begin with 46 and repeatedly subtract 10.

PROBLEM 84   Put a single digit in each box and make the problem correct:

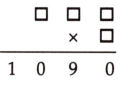

Discussion   There are 2 possible answers:

$$
\begin{array}{r}
545 \\
\times\ \ 2 \\
\hline
1090
\end{array}
\qquad
\begin{array}{r}
218 \\
\times\ \ 5 \\
\hline
1090
\end{array}
$$

PROBLEM 85   How much will it cost to cut a log into 8 equal pieces if cutting it into 4 equal pieces costs 60¢ ? There is no stacking of pieces.

Discussion   Make a drawing of the log. It is easy to see that cutting the log into 4 pieces requires only 3 cuts. Thus, each cut costs 20¢. To cut the log into 8 equal pieces we need only 7 cuts at 20¢ each, or $1.40.

PROBLEM 86   With 3 minutes left to play in the game between the Cougars and the Hawks, the Cougars were ahead by 10 points. In those last 3 minutes, however, the Cougars scored 6 points per minute, while the Hawks scored 9 points per minute. Who won the game and by how many points?

Discussion   Examine the score during those last 3 minutes. The Cougars scored 3 × 6 or 18 points. The Hawks scored 3 × 9 or 27 points. The Hawks scored 9 points more than the Cougars, but they had trailed by 10 points. Thus the Cougars won by 1 point. An alternate method might be to pick any scores with the Cougars ahead by 10 points, say 48 to 38. In 3 minutes, the Hawks scored 3 × 9 or 27 points. Their final score will be 38 + 27 or 65. But the Cougars scored 3 × 6 or 18 points, so their final score will be 48 + 18 or 66, so the Cougars won by 1 point.

PROBLEM 87   Mitchell just bought a new car. Lester said it was a blue Dodge. Patricia said it was a black Chevrolet. Sandy said it was a black Ford. If each person correctly identified either the make of the car or its color but not both, what was the actual color and make of Mitchell's new car?

Discussion   Use logic. If the car had been blue (Lester's choice), then both Sandy and Patricia would have the color wrong and the car would have to be both a Chevrolet and a Ford. This is, of course, impossible. Thus, Lester was wrong about the color and right about the make. The car was a Dodge. Therefore, both Sandy and Patricia were correct in naming the color as black. The car as a black Dodge.

PROBLEM 88   Which of the following sums of money could you pay with exactly 3 coins? Tell how you would do it.

7¢   16¢   22¢   56¢

Discussion   Give the children several pennies, nickels, dimes, quarters, and half-dollars, or chips and tokens that are appropriately marked. Have them experiment until they find the proper combinations.

$$7¢ = 5¢ + 1¢ + 1¢$$
$$16¢ = 10¢ + 5¢ + 1¢$$
$$56¢ = 50¢ + 5¢ + 1¢$$

PROBLEM 89   Fill in the squares with the numbers 2, 3, or 4 so that the numbers in each row (across, down, and diagonally) add up to 9.

3	4	
		3

Discussion   This is an exercise working with number facts. Horizontally, we have 3 + 4 = 7; thus we need a 2 for a sum of 9. Now we add vertically in the right-hand column, 2 + 3 = 5; thus we need a 4 in the missing box. Continue in a similar manner. (Note: Several correct answers are possible.)

PROBLEM 90   A city block is about 270 feet long. Cars are parked bumper-to-bumper; a small car is 15 feet long and a large car is 18 feet long.

(a) What is the smallest number of cars that can be parked in 1 block?
(b) What is the largest number of cars that can be parked in 1 block?
(c) If we park an equal number of large and small cars in 1 block, how many would fit?

Discussion   (a) The smallest number of cars occurs when all the cars are large cars. 270 ÷ 18 = 15. The smallest number of cars is 15 cars.
(b) The largest number of cars occurs when all the cars are small ones. 270 ÷ 15 = 18. The largest number of cars is 18 cars.
(c) Since there are an equal number of each size, a pair of cars will total 15 + 18 or 33 feet. 270 ÷ 33 = 8.1 There will be 8 cars of each size parked on the block.

Since 270 is the product of 18 and 15, parts (a) and (b) can be done mentally.

PROBLEM 91   Gail bought 5 pencils that cost 12¢ each and 3 erasers that cost 8¢ each. She gave the clerk a $1 bill. How much change did she get?

Discussion   This is another example of a multi-stage problem that should be done by the divide and conquer strategy. Work the problem carefully in stages.
Stage 1: 5 pencils = 5 × 12¢ = 60¢
Stage 2: 3 erasers = 3 × 8¢ = 24¢
Stage 3: Amount spent–60¢ + 24¢ = 84¢
Stage 4: $1.00 – .84-16¢
She received 16¢ in change.

PROBLEM 92   You had 7 dimes and 7 pennies. You bought a comic book for 49¢. You give the clerk 5 coins and she gives you 1 coin back. What coins do you now have?

Discussion   Some children will need the actual coins to solve this problem. Others may simulate the situation with a paper and pencil. There is only one way to pay 49¢ and receive one coin in change, and that is with 5 dimes from which you get 1¢ in change. Thus, you now have 2 dimes and 8 pennies.

PROBLEM 93   Each vehicle that crosses the Banana River Toll Bridge must pay $1.50 per axle. A large trailer truck has 18 wheels. There are 2 wheels on the front axle, and 4 wheels on each of the other axles. How much must the truck driver pay to cross the river by the toll bridge?

Discussion   Divide and conquer. Use manipulatives if necessary. 18 wheels minus 2 (the number on the front axle) yields 16. 16 divided by 4 (the number on each of the other axles) tells us that there are 4 additional axles. The total number of axles is 5, and the driver must pay 5 × $1.50 or $7.50 to cross the river by the toll bridge.

PROBLEM 94

3 yuchs = 2 ughs
4 ughs = 6 wims
2 yucks = ? wims

Discussion

3 yucks = 2 ughs
6 yuchs = 4 ughs = 6 wims

If 6 yuchs = 6 wims, then 2 yuchs will equal 2 wims.

171

PROBLEM 95   There are 5 students in Mrs. Martin's class who wish to ride on a bicycle built for 2. How many rides must they take so that each person rides with each other person just one time?

Discussion   Make an organized list of all the possible pairs of students:

A-B	B-C	C-D	D-E
A-C	B-D	C-E	
A-D	B-E		
A-E			

There will be 10 rides needed. Notice that this list exhausts all the possible ways in which the rides can be taken. The list does not include *B-A*, since *A-B* and *B-A* are the same two students. This is typical of the combinatorial problems that students will encounter later in their mathematics program.

PROBLEM 96   Rex tossed five number cubes. All the cubes have three 4's and three 5's on them.

(a) What is the smallest sum that Rex could obtain by adding the faces that are up?
(b) What is the largest sum that Rex could obtain by adding the faces that are up?
(c) Rex added up his score and got a 22. How many 4's and how many 5's were there?

Discussion   Give the students five cubes numbered as the problem stated. Have them arrange their cubes to find the smallest sum, the largest sum, and a sum of 22. The smallest sum possible is 20 (5 × 4). The largest sum is 25 (5 × 5). To obtain a 22, we need three 4's and two 5's. Some children may not need the physical aid of the actual cubes—they can solve the problem mentally.

PROBLEM 97   What is the greatest number of coins you can use to make 35¢? What is the smallest number of coins you can use? In how many different ways can you make 35¢?

Discussion   The greatest number of coins is obviously 35 pennies. The smallest number of coins is 2 (1 dime and 1 quarter). To find the number of *different* ways change can be made, we can make a table:

Pennies	Nickels	Dimes	Quarters
35	—	—	—
30	1	—	—
25	—	1	—
25	2	—	—
.	.	.	.
.	.	.	.
.	.	.	.
—	—	1	1

PROBLEM 98   John was counting the number of tops he had in each of his colored boxes. There were 5 tops in the yellow box. There were 7 tops altogether in the red and white boxes. There were 6 tops altogether in the red and blue boxes. There were 7 tops altogether in the yellow and blue boxes. How many tops were in the white box? How many tops were there altogether?

Discussion   Fact #1 establishes 5 tops in the yellow box. This, together with the fourth fact, establishes that there are 2 tops in the blue box. This and fact #3 tells us that there are 4 tops in the red box. This and the second fact establish that there are 3 tops in the white box and 14 tops altogether.

PROBLEM 99   How many breaths do you take in a 24-hour day?

Discussion   Have the students first determine how many breaths they take in 1 minute. Then use a calculator. Multiply by 60 (to find the number of breaths in 1 hour) and then by 24 (for 1 day). For example, if a student takes 20 breaths in 1 minute, he or she would take 20 × 60 × 24 or 28,800 breaths in one day. Students may be amazed at the size of the final answer.

PROBLEM 100   On the new TV game show, each question is worth 3 times as much as the previous question. The fifth question on the show is worth $405. What is the first question worth?

Discussion   Work backwards. Since the fifth question is worth $405, the fourth question is worth $135. The third question is then worth $45, the second is worth $15, and the first question is worth $5.

PROBLEM 101   Five bookworms have eaten into the big dictionary on the teacher's desk. Twiggy is 20 mm ahead of Rusty. Cruncher is 10 mm behind Twiggy. Rusty is 5 mm behind Nosey. Freddy is 15 mm ahead of Cruncher. Nosey is 20 mm behind Freddy. List the positions of the 5 bookworms in order.

Discussion

Draw a number line and use the clues to place the book-worms on the line. (The bookworms are chewing from right to left.)

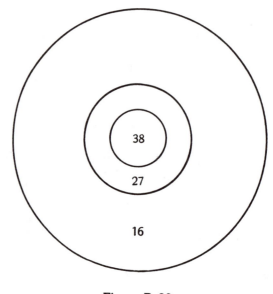

Notice that the final clue (Nosey is 20 mm behind Freddy), is not needed to solve the problem. However, it does help us check our work.

PROBLEM 102

You get 2 tosses with a beanbag at the target shown in Figure B–20. How many different possible scores can you get? What are they?

Figure B–20

Discussion

Make an exhaustive list of all possible scores. Organize your list to be certain that you have all possible scores.

16 + 16 = 32	27 + 27 = 54	38 + 38 = 76
16 + 27 = 43	27 + 38 = 65	
16 + 38 = 54		

Notice that there are 2 different ways to score 54. We must only count 1 of these. Thus, there are 5 different scores possible: 76, 65, 54, 43, 32.

PROBLEM 103   How long is a row of 24 pennies placed side by side so that they touch?

Discussion   Take 24 pennies. Place them side by side as shown in Figure B–21. Measure the length of the line with a ruler. Some students might measure 1 penny and multiply by 24. This could reveal a slight error or difference in the answer due to an error of precision in measuring the penny. The line should be about 18 inches long.

Figure B–21

PROBLEM 104   Jeff's plant is shorter than Nancy's. Danny's plant is taller than Nancy's. Jeff's plant is taller than Brad's. Whose plant is the tallest? Whose is the shortest?

Discussion   Vertical line segments representing each person's plant, as in Figure B–22, will enable the students to discover that Danny's plant is the tallest and Brad's plant is the shortest.

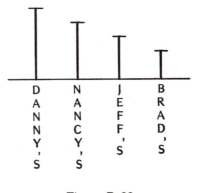

Figure B–22

PROBLEM 105   Mrs. Miller wants to buy 27 prehistoric model figures so that she can give 1 to each student in her class. She can buy model dinosaurs that come 4 in a box, and she can buy the model cavemen singly. In how many different ways can she buy the 27 models?

Discussion   Make a table:

Dinosaurs		Cavemen
Boxes	Number	Number
1	4	23
2	8	19
3	12	15
4	16	11
5	20	7
6	24	3

She can buy the models in 6 different ways.

PROBLEM 106   The Little League box scores appeared on 2 facing pages of the local newspaper. The sum of the page numbers is 13. What are the page numbers?

Discussion   Students must realize that the numbers on 2 facing pages of a newspaper are consecutive, with the lower number on the left-side page. List all possible number pairs of successive integers and find the pair whose sum is 13 (pages 6 and 7). It is possible that some students may find the "average" page number ($13 \div 2 = 6\frac{1}{2}$) and then use the actual page numbers on either side of $6\frac{1}{2}$, namely 6 and 7.

PROBLEM 107   For each of the following, an answer has been given. Tell whether the answer given is reasonable. If not, tell why not.

(a) Maureen bought a hamburger for $1.29, french fries for 79¢, and a small soft drink for 86¢. What is her change from a $10 bill? (Answer: $4.50)

(b) At the ball game last evening, there were 6,987 people in attendance. The park holds 72,000 people when filled to capacity. How many empty seats were there last night? (Answer: about 65,000)

(c) A parking garage can park 126 cars on each of its 4 floors. How many cars can the garage hold when it is full? (Answer: about 800)

(d) The local pet shop just received a shipment of 3,556 tropical fish. They put the fish into groups of 40 in large quarantine tanks for 3 days. About how many quarantine tanks are there? (Answer: about 90 tanks)

Discussion   These problems require the students to practice their estimation skills. They are not to solve the problems, simply to decide if the answer given is a reasonable one. In (a), the answer is not reasonable, since a hamburger, french fries and the drink cost *about* $3. Maureen's change should be about $7. In (b), there were *about* 7,000 people in attendance, so the answer is a reasonable one. In (c), the garage holds *about* 4 × 125 or 500 cars when full; thus 800 is not reasonable. In (d), 90 × 40 is 3,600; the answer is reasonable.

PROBLEM 108   Melinda bought some peanuts for 35¢ and an apple for 20¢. She paid for her purchase with 3 coins of the same amount. How much change did she receive?

Discussion   When we add 35¢ and 20¢ we get 55¢. Melinda could not have paid her bill with 3 nickels (15¢) or 3 dimes (30¢). She would not have paid with 3 half-dollars, since 2 would have been enough. Thus, she must have paid with 3 quarters or 75¢. Her change was 75¢ – 55¢ = 20¢.

PROBLEM 109   Given the sequence of numbers

$$2, \quad 3, \quad 5, \quad 8$$

explain why the next number might be 12, or 13, or 2, or 5.

Discussion   There are many ways in which the four given terms might have been arrived at. For example, if we regard these as members of a Fibonacci sequence, each term was arrived at by adding the previous two terms. Thus, 2 + 3 = 5, 3 + 5 = 8, 5 + 8 = 13, and so on. On the other hand, we might view the sequence as having been generated by adding increasing differences. Thus, 2 + 1 = 3, 3 + 2 = 5, 5 + 3 = 8, 8 + 4 = 12, and so on. Also, the sequence might be viewed as a cyclical sequence in which the four terms repeat. Thus the next term would again be a 2. Finally, the sequence might be a 7-term series that is symmetrical about the middle term, 8. Thus the next term would be 5.

PROBLEM 110   At which step do you go over 100 ?

Step 1	Step 2	Step 3	Step 4
1	2	4	8
+ 1	+ 2	+ 4	+ 8

177

Discussion	Use a calculator. Students should continue the pattern until they reach the step where the answer becomes a 3-digit number. Step 5 is 16 + 16 = 32; Step 6 is 32 + 32 = 64; Step 7 is 64 + 64 = 128, which is over 100.
PROBLEM 111	At the fair, Janet and Mike were guessing how many corks were in a large jar. Mike guessed that there were 850 corks. The barker told him that he was off by 150 corks. Janet guessed that there were 1,100 corks. The barker told her that she, too, was off, but only by 100 corks. How many corks are in the jar?
Discussion	Mike's guess of 850 corks was off by 150. Therefore, there were either 700 or 1,000 corks in the jar. Janet was off by 100, thus there were either 1,000 or 1,200 corks. There must have been 1,000 corks in the jar.
PROBLEM 112	The listed price for *Sports Magazine* is $1.25 a copy. You pay $16.56 for a 24-issue subscription. How much do you save by buying the subscription?
Discussion	This is an example of a 2-stage problem. Students must first find the total cost of 24 copies at the per-issue rate of $1.25. Then they subtract the subscription price from this total to find the amount they save.
PROBLEM 113	Marianne is a guard on the school basketball team. Her season's average for the first 6 games was 8 points per game. Tonight she scored 15 points. What is her new average?
Discussion	Work backwards. If Marianne's average for 6 games was 8 points per game, then her total points scored was $8 \times 6 = 48$ points. Her new total is 48 + 15 or 63 points in 9 games. Thus her average was $\frac{63}{9}$ or 7 points per game.
PROBLEM 114	There were 8 girls and 16 boys at a meeting of the June Fair planning committee of the third grade. Every few minutes, 1 boy and 1 girl leave the meeting to go back to class. How many of these boy and girl pairs must leave the meeting so that there will be exactly 5 times as many boys as girls at the meeting?
Discussion	Make a list.

Boys	Girls	
16	8	
15	7	
14	6	
13	5	
12	4	
11	3	
10	2	(This is a 5:1 ratio.)

Six pairs must leave to reach the 5:1 ratio of boys to girls.

PROBLEM 115   Figure B–23 shows designs drawn on the 6 faces of a cube.

Figure B–23

Figure B–24 contains 3 views of the same cube showing some of the faces. Which designs are on opposite faces of the cube?

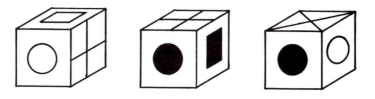

Figure B–24

Discussion   From the second and third views of the cube, we can see that neither the + sign, the solid square, the X, nor the open circle can be *opposite* the solid circle, since they are all shown to be *adjacent* to the solid circle. Therefore, only the open square can be opposite the solid circle. In a similar manner, it can be shown that the open circle is opposite the solid square and the + is opposite the X.

PROBLEM 116   Laura jogged 7 blocks on the first day she started her training program. She increased her distance by 2 blocks each day. On the last day, she jogged 25 blocks. How many days was she in training?

Discussion   Make an organized list.

Day	Number of Blocks
1	7
2	9
3	11
4	13
.	.
.	.
.	.
11	25

PROBLEM 117   See Figure B–25. One clock is 20 minutes fast. One clock is 15 minutes slow. One clock is 5 minutes fast. One clock is exactly right. What is the correct time?

Figure B–25

Discussion Use logic and guess and test. Since 1 clock is 20 minutes fast and 1 is 15 minutes slow, the correct time must lie between the 2 extreme times, namely between 2:35 and 2:00. The correct time is 2:15.

PROBLEM 118 Janine had 5 coins: quarters, nickels and dimes. The total value of her coins was 50¢. How many of each coin did she have?

Discussion Make an exhaustive list.

Quarters	Dimes	Nickels	Total	Number of Coins
2	0	0	50¢	2
1	2	1	50¢	4
1	1	3	50¢	5
0	5	0	50¢	5
0	4	2	50¢	6
0	3	4	50¢	7
0	2	6	50¢	8
0	1	8	50¢	9
0	0	10	50¢	10

Since Janine had some of all 3 kinds of coins, only the combination of 1 quarter, 1 dime, and 3 nickels will satisfy the given conditions.

PROBLEM 119 On an assembly line that paints stripes around glass paperweights, there are 3 stations. The first station paints a red stripe on every third paperweight. The second station paints a green stripe on every fourth paperweight. The third station paints a blue stripe on every sixth paperweight. The machine produced 100 paperweights yesterday. How many of these had all 3 stripes on them?

Discussion Make a table.

Red	3	6	9	12	15	18	21	24	27	30	...

Green	4	8	12	16	20	24	28	32	36	40	...

Blue	6	12	18	24	30	36	42	48	...

Students should see the pattern, numbers 12, 24, 36, . . ., 96. Thus there are 8 paperweights with all 3 stripes. In problem

77, whose solution is similar, the numbers were relatively prime, so all we needed was their product. Here, however, the 3, 4, and 6 are *not* relatively prime, so we must use prime factorization; i.e.,

$$3 = 1 \times 3$$
$$4 = 2 \times 2$$
$$6 = 3 \times 2$$

Thus the LCM is $2 \times 2 \times 3 = 12$.

PROBLEM 120

The Clarks are planning a barbecue for the holiday weekend. They have invited 12 people. Morrie wants to serve the chicken at 6:30 P.M. The charcoal must burn for 20 to 30 minutes before he places the chickens on the grill. He plans to barbecue the chickens for 30 to 40 minutes before serving them. When should he start the charcoal?

Discussion

Work backwards. if Morrie wants to serve the chickens at 6:30 P.M., he should begin cooking the chickens between 5:50 and 6:00 (40 and 30 minutes, respectively). Since the charcoal must burn for 20 to 30 minutes, he should light the charcoal between 5:20 and 5:30. To be *certain* he can serve the chicken at exactly 6:30 P.M., he should start the charcoal at 5:20 P.M.

PROBLEM 121

The advance registration for next week's music camp shows a total of 72 campers who have registered so far. To be certain that the classes are kept small, Mr. Marcus, the camp director, wants to hire a sufficient number of teachers. He has already hired 9 teachers. How many more should he hire?

Discussion

This problem has insufficient information; it cannot be solved. Have the children supply a *reasonable* number for the students in each class, and then solve the problem. Use the divide and conquer strategy.

PROBLEM 122

A taxi charges 90¢ for the first one-fifth of a mile, and 25¢ for each additional fifth of a mile. Sandy paid $2.90 for her ride. How far did she travel?

Discussion

Sandy spent 90¢ of the $2.90 for the first one-fifth of a mile. The remaining $2.00, when divided by 25¢ for each fifth of a mile, yields 8 additional fifths of miles. Thus, she paid for a ride of $\frac{9}{5}$ miles, or $1\frac{4}{5}$ miles. Note: Since the meter "clicks" at the beginning of a one-fifth segment, the actual ride must have been somewhere between $1\frac{3}{5}$ miles and $1\frac{4}{5}$ miles. (This problem is typical of a class of problems whose graph yields a step-function. Other problems in this class include postage rates, sales tax, etc.)

PROBLEM 123

In a school supply store, 1 pencil and 3 erasers cost 90¢. Two pencils and 2 erasers cost $1.00. Three pencils and 1 eraser cost $1.10. How much does 1 eraser cost? How much does 1 pencil cost?

Discussion

Of course there is an algebraic solution for this problem, but this is beyond the level of this book. Use logic and guess and test. Start with a pencil that costs 10¢. That leaves 80¢ for 3 erasers, but 80 is not divisible by 3. Try 15¢ for a pencil. This makes the cost of an eraser 25¢, but this does not satisfy the second fact. Continue until you arrive at the answers: 30¢ for a pencil and 20¢ for an eraser.

PROBLEM 124

I have two children. The product of their ages is 24. The sum of their ages is 11. Find the ages of my children.

Discussion

Make a list of all pairs of numbers whose product is 24.

$$24 \times 1$$
$$12 \times 2$$
$$8 \times 3$$
$$6 \times 4$$

Now find which of these pairs has a sum of 11. The children's ages are 8 and 3.

PROBLEM 125

How many more three-digit numbers are there than two-digit numbers?

Discussion

From 10 through 99, there are 90 two-digit numbers.
From 100 through 999, there are 900 three-digit numbers.
Thus there are 810 more three-digit numbers than two-digit numbers.

PROBLEM 126   What is the sum of all the numbers in this table?

$\frac{3}{4}$	$\frac{3}{8}$	$\frac{3}{7}$	$\frac{3}{5}$	$\frac{3}{13}$
$\frac{2}{5}$	$\frac{4}{7}$	$\frac{10}{13}$	$\frac{5}{8}$	$\frac{1}{4}$

Discussion   A careful examination of the table reveals that there are 5 pairs of fractions and each pair has a sum of 1. Thus, the sum of the 10 numbers is 5.

PROBLEM 127   What was the final score of the Tigers-Sharks baseball game?

(a) If their scores are added, the sum is 8.
(b) If their scores are multiplied, the product is 15.
(c) The Sharks won the game.

Discussion   Make a list of all the number pairs whose sum is 8:

$$8 + 0$$
$$7 + 1$$
$$6 + 2$$
$$5 + 3$$
$$4 + 4$$

Now, find the pair of numbers on the list whose product is 15. Since the Sharks won the game, the final score must have been Sharks 5, Tigers 3.

PROBLEM 128   Every night, Janet's dad puts all of his nickels, dimes, and quarters into a box. At the end of the month, he deposits the coins in the bank. Last month he deposited exactly $10. Janet noticed that he had the same number of nickels, dimes, and quarters. How many of each coin did her dad deposit in the bank?

Discussion   Use guess and test, together with an organized list. He deposited 25 of each coin.

PROBLEM 129   Pat and Mike are having a contest. They will shovel snow to clear a 21-foot path. Pat shovels 3 feet with each push of the shovel. Mike shovels 1 foot on the first push, 2 feet on the second push, 3 feet on the third push, and so on; he shovels 1 foot more on each push than on the push before. Who wins the contest?

Discussion   Make a table to simulate the action.

Pat			Mike	
Total Distance	Per-Push Distance	Push Number	Per-Push Distance	Total Distance
3	3	1	1	1
6	3	2	2	3
9	3	3	3	6
12	3	4	4	10
15	3	5	5	15
18	3	6	6	21

Mike wins the contest, since he shoveled the 21 feet on the sixth push, while Pat had only shoveled 18 feet.

PROBLEM 130

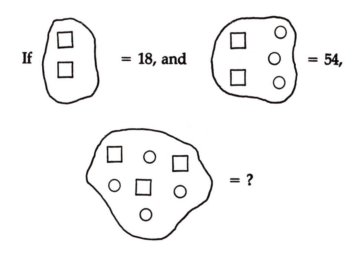

Discussion   If 2 squares = 18, then each square = 9. Thus, 3 circles + 18 will equal 54 and each circle = 12. Then 3 squares plus 4 circles will equal 3(9) + 4(12) = 27 + 48 = 75.

PROBLEM 131   In a local restaurant, a circular table seats 4 people. A rectangular table seats 6 people. There are 18 people waiting to be seated. How can it be done?

Discussion   Make a list of the multiples of 4 and a list of the multiples of 6. See what numbers in both lists can be added to give a sum of 18.

Multiples of 4	Multiples of 6
4	6
8	12
12	18
16	

Three tables of 6 or 3 tables of 4 and 1 table of 6 are the answers.

PROBLEM 132   One paper clip is 3 centimeters long and weighs $1\frac{1}{2}$ grams. Joan made a chain of these paper clips that was 360 centimeters long. How many grams did the chain weigh?

Discussion   Find the number of paper clips by dividing 360 centimeters by 3 centimeters. There are 120 clips in the chain. To find their total weight, multiply the number of clips by the weight of each clip.

PROBLEM 133   Here is a menu for lunch in school:

Hamburger	68¢
French fries	35¢
Malted milk	55¢
Milk	25¢

James spent $1.28 for lunch. What did he buy?

Discussion   By guess and test we arrive at 1 hamburger, 1 french fries, and 1 milk. (Ask the students if other answers are possible). The fact that only 1 item on the menu ends with an 8 helps a great deal.

PROBLEM 134   Alim, Brenda, and Carol sold fruit at the school carnival. They sold oranges, apples, and pears.

(a) Alim and the orange seller are sisters.
(b) The apple seller is older than Brenda.
(c) Carol sold the pears.

Who sold each kind of fruit?

Discussion   Clue (c) tells us that Carol sold the pears. Since Alim cannot be the orange seller (from clue (a)), she sold the apples. Thus, Brenda sold the oranges.

PROBLEM 135   David has been raising tomatoes to sell at his roadside stand. He decides to put them into small baskets to sell. When he puts them into the baskets by 3's, he has 2 left over. If he puts them into the basket by 4's, he has 3 left over. If he knows that he has fewer than 100 tomatoes, how many might he have?

Discussion   Make two lists, one of 3's with 2 left over and one by 4's with 3 left over:

By 3's	5, 8, (11), 14, 17, 20, (23), 26, 29, 32, (35), . . .
By 4's	7, (11), 15, 19, (23), 27, 31, (35), 39, . . .

He might have had 11, 23, 35, 47, 59, 71, 83, or 95 tomatoes. Notice that these numbers are all odd. Why?

PROBLEM 136   There are 4 boats sailing on the river in a straight line. The yellow boat is in front of the red boat. The blue boat is behind the green boat. The yellow boat is behind the blue boat. In what order are the boats?

Discussion   Draw a line. Place the boats on the line according to the clues, one at a time:

$$\text{R} \quad \text{Y} \quad \text{B} \quad \text{G}$$

PROBLEM 137   A triangular shape of grapefruit is placed on the window shelf in a local supermarket. The display is made by placing a row of grapefruit on the shelf and then a row containing 1 less grapefruit on top of that row. Continue in this way until 1 grapefruit is on the top row. If a total of 21 grapefruit is used, how many rows are in the triangular display?

Discussion   Work backwards. Start with the top row of 1 grapefruit. If there were only one row, there would be only 1 block. Make a table.

Number of Rows	Total Number of Grapefruit
1	1 = 1
2	1 + 2 = 3
3	1 + 2 + 3 = 6
4	1 + 2 + 3 + 4 = 10
5	1 + 2 + 3 + 4 + 5 = 15
6	1 + 2 + 3 + 4 + 5 + 6 = 21

There are 6 rows in the display. Notice that this problem can easily be extended. What if there were 55 grapefruit? 91 grapefruit?

PROBLEM 138   Nicole has a package of 48 silver stars. She wants to arrange them in rows, so that each row has the same number of stars. How can she arrange them so that the number of stars in each row is an odd number?

Discussion   Have the children make a list of all the number pairs whose product is 48:

Number of Rows	×	Number of Stars
48	×	1
24	×	2
16	×	3
12	×	4
8	×	6
6	×	8
4	×	12
3	×	16
2	×	24
1	×	48

There are only 2 sets of numbers where the number of stars in each row is an odd number, namely 48 rows of 1 star and 16 rows of 3 stars.

PROBLEM 139 How many lengths of rope, each 3 feet long, can be cut from a coil that contains 50 feet of rope?

Discussion If we divide 50 by 3, we obtain 16 with a remainder of 2. Thus the correct answer is 16. Disregard the remainder, since we need each length to be exactly 3 feet long.

PROBLEM 140 A farmer has 15 animals, some of them pigs and some chickens. Together they have a total of 40 legs. How many pigs and how many chickens does the farmer have?

Discussion We have the restriction that pigs have 4 legs and chickens have 2 legs each. Guess and test. Prepare a table to record our guesses and to refine each guess as we proceed.

Pigs	Legs	Chickens	Legs	Total Number of Legs
1	4	14	28	32
2	8	13	26	34
3	12	12	24	36
4	16	11	22	38
5	20	10	20	40

The farmer had 5 pigs and 10 chickens.

PROBLEM 141

> **Table of Moon Facts**
> The moon is smaller than the Earth.
> People weigh 6 times as much on Earth as on the moon.
> The moon goes around the Earth once every 28 days.
> The moon is about 240,000 miles from Earth.

(a) Peter figures that he would weigh 14 pounds on the moon. What does Peter weigh on Earth?
(b) Peter's mother weighs 120 pounds on Earth. How much would she weigh on the moon?
(c) About how long does it take the moon to go around the Earth 4 times?

Discussion This 3-part problem involves obtaining facts from a table.

(a) If Peter weighs 14 pounds on the moon, he must weigh 84 pounds on Earth.

(b) If Peter's mother weighs 120 pounds on Earth, she would weigh $\frac{1}{6}$ as much, or 20 pounds, on the moon.

(c) If the moon goes around the earth once in 28 days, it would take approximately 112 days to go around the Earth 4 times.

PROBLEM 142

Half of the boys and girls who went to the fair ate ice cream. Half of the remaining girls ate popcorn. No boys ate popcorn. Altogether, 20 boys and 40 girls went to the fair. How many children ate neither ice cream nor popcorn?

Discussion

Make a table.

	20 Boys	40 Girls
Ice Cream	10	20
Popcorn	—	10
Total	10	30

Thus, there were 10 boys and 10 girls who ate neither ice cream nor popcorn.

PROBLEM 143

A fancy bottle of perfume costs $25. The bottle alone, without the perfume, can be purchased by collectors. When purchased this way, the bottle alone costs $15 less than the perfume alone. How much does the bottle alone cost?

Discussion

Guess and test provides an alternative to an algebraic solution. Since the total for the bottle and perfume was $25, one could guess $1 for the bottle, which leaves $24 for the perfume. Using an organized list to keep track of the guesses is an important skill.

Bottle	Perfume	Total
$1	$24	$25
2	23	25
3	22	25
4	21	25
5	20	25

The bottle alone costs $5.

PROBLEM 144

"I want you to go shopping for me," said Jimmy's mother. "First of all, go 5 blocks west to the grocery store. Then go 3 blocks east to the fruit store. Then go 5 blocks east to the candy store." Which store is closest to Jimmy's house?

Discussion

Simulate the action with a series of drawings of a number line. (See Figure B–26.)

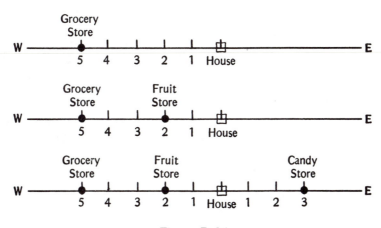

Figure B–26

PROBLEM 145

The Boy Scout troop earns money for charity by painting house numbers on the curb in front of each house. They receive 75¢ for each digit they paint. The house numbers begin with 1, then go up one number at a time: 2, 3, 4, ... When they were finished, they had earned $128.25. How many house numbers did they paint?

Discussion

If they earned $128.75, and each digit was 75¢, they must have painted 171 digits. The first 9 houses used up 9 of them, leaving 162 digits, or 81 houses. Thus there were 81 + 9, or 90 houses.

PROBLEM 146

Alexandra baked some chocolate chip cookies last Thursday. She gave 10 of them to her friend, Nancy. Then she gave half of the rest to her sister, Helen. Her father took 7 of the ones that were left. Alexandra then ate half of the rest and put the last 10 cookies away for her mother. How many cookies did she bake originally?

Discussion

Work backwards. Since there were 10 cookies to put away when Alexandra ate half, there must have been 20 cookies. Her father took 7, so there were 27. Helen received half, so there were 54. Nancy took 10, so there must have been 64 to start.

PROBLEM 147

Mrs. Lewis bought 6 greeting cards. Mr. Lewis bought 6 cards that same day. How much would they have saved if they had bought the 12 cards together?

Number of Cards	1–3	4–6	7–9	10–12	13 or more
Cost for Each Card	$1.00	90¢	85¢	80¢	75¢

Discussion

The necessary information for obtaining the answer is in the table. First find the cost for each person to buy 6 cards:

$$6 \times 90¢ = \$5.40$$

They spent a total of $10.80 for their 12 cards. Now find the cost for 12 cards made as a single purchase:

$$12 \times 80¢ = \$9.60$$

They would have saved $10.80 – $9.60 or $1.20.

PROBLEM 148

Tanya has a 5-room apartment where all the rooms lie in a straight line. The bedroom is next to the kitchen. The living room is between the kitchen and the dining room. The recreation room is farthest from the bedroom. Which room is in the middle?

Discussion

Make a drawing to show the given information.

| Bedroom | Kitchen | Living Room | Dining Room | Recreation Room |

The living room is in the middle.

PROBLEM 149

The big clock in the hall loses 5 minutes every hour. David set the clock at exactly 8:00 A.M. when he left for school. He came back at exactly 4:00 P.M.. What time did the big clock show?

Discussion

David was away for 7 hours. During that time, the clock lost 7 × 5 or 35 minutes. The clock must have read 3:25.

PROBLEM 150

A rabbit ate 32 carrots in 4 days. If he ate 2 more carrots each day than he did the day before, how many carrots did he eat on each day?

Discussion	Guess and test. Some children may require hands-on materials. Give them 32 tokens, chips, or other materials. Have them separate the chips into 4 piles, each of which contains 2 more chips than the preceding one. The answer is 5 the first day, 7 the second day, 9 the third day, and 11 carrots the fourth day.

PROBLEM 151	Dan has a bad cold and has to take 1 teaspoon of cough syrup every $2\frac{1}{2}$ hours. He took his first dose at 9:00 A.M. He is supposed to take 6 doses before he goes to bed at 8:00 P.M. Can he do it?

Discussion	Make a table showing the time at which Dan takes each dose. The table reveals the answer.

Time	Dose Number
9:00	1
11:30	2
2:00	3
4:30	4
7:00	5
9:30	6

He cannot take the sixth dose in time before he goes to bed.

PROBLEM 152	The Forest Rangers are giving away 960 blue spruce saplings to be used in a reforestation project. The Jones Middle School is helping with the planting. They gave $\frac{1}{4}$ of the plants to the fifth grade class and $\frac{1}{2}$ of that amount to the sixth grade class. The seventh grade class received $\frac{1}{2}$ of what was left, and the eighth grade class received $\frac{1}{4}$ of that number. They kept the plants that were left for next year's replacements. How many plants were left?

Discussion	Make a table.

Given Away	Remaining
—	960
240	720
120	600
300	300
75	225

There were 225 saplings left.

PROBLEM 153   The cost of a concert ticket and a football ticket is $14. The cost of a movie ticket and a football ticket is $11. The cost of a concert ticket and a movie ticket is $7. Find the cost of each ticket.

Discussion   A concert ticket and a football ticket cost $14. A movie ticket and a football ticket cost $11. Thus, the concert ticket is $3 more than the movie ticket. Since the concert ticket and the movie ticket together cost $7, we need two numbers whose sum is 7 and whose difference is 3. Guess and test. The concert ticket cost $5; the football ticket costs $9; the movie ticket costs $2.

PROBLEM 154   Norene set her wristwatch when she left for school at exactly 7:30 A.M. on Monday. At 1:30 P.M. on Monday, she noticed that her watch had lost 4 minutes. At this same rate, how many minutes will the watch lose by the time Norene resets it when she leaves for school at 7:30 A.M. on Tuesday?

Discussion   Although this problem can be solved by many students by counting, since clock arithmetic is in base 12, others may need a picture of a clock or a model of a clock with movable hands to illustrate the situation. From the drawing, students should see that the elapsed time between 7:30 A.M. and 1:30 P.M. is 6 hours. Since there are 24 hours until 7:30 A.M. on Tuesday, we need a number 4 times the 6 hours. Thus, 4 times 4 minutes will mean that her watch loses 16 minutes.

PROBLEM 155   Karen has 3 different teachers for science, mathematics, and music. Mrs. Alexander enjoys her work as a music teacher. Mr. Brown used to teach science, but doesn't anymore. Mrs. Carlton was absent last Tuesday. Who teaches each subject?

Discussion   Use logic The first clue establishes Mrs. Alexander as the music teacher. The second clue tells us that Mr. Brown is not the science teacher, and therefore must be the mathematics teacher. Notice that the third clue is not needed.

PROBLEM 156   At the record store, Carol bought the same number of tapes as records. She bought the same number of Western records as all the other records she bought. How many records and how many tapes did she buy if she bought 5 Western records?

Discussion   Work backwards. Carol bought 5 Western records; thus, she bought 5 other records as well, or 10 records altogether. Since she also bought the same number of tapes (10) as records, her total was 20 records and tapes.

PROBLEM 157   Maureen brought an apple, an orange, and a peach to her science class. She weighed them 2 at a time. The apple and the orange weighed 14 ounces; the apple and the peach weighed 18 ounces; the orange and the peach weighed 18 ounces. How much did the apple weigh?

Discussion   The apple and the orange weighed 14 ounces. The apple and the peach weighed 18 ounces. This tells us that the peach weighs 4 ounces more than the orange. However, the orange and the peach together weigh 20 ounces. Thus we are looking for two numbers whose sum is 20 and which differ by 4, namely 8 and 12. The weights turn out to be: the orange = 8 ounces; the peach = 12 ounces; the apple = 6 ounces.

PROBLEM 158   Mary bought a candy bar for 29¢. She gave the clerk a $1 bill and received 5 coins in change. What 5 coins did she receive?

Discussion   Since she gave the clerk $1 and spent 29¢, she must have received 71¢ in change. Make an exhaustive list showing all the possibilities. Notice that she obviously received 1¢, leaving 4 coins to make 70¢.

50¢	25¢	10¢	5¢	1¢
1	—	1	2	1
—	2	2	—	1

She received either 2 quarters, 2 dimes, and 1 penny, or she received 1 half-dollar, 1 dime, 2 nickels, and 1 penny.

PROBLEM 159   Stanley makes extra money by buying and selling old comic books. He buys them for 85¢ each and sells them for $1.00 each. Stanley needs $19.50 to buy a new calculator. How many comic books must he buy and sell to earn the $19.50?

Discussion   Some students will realize that Stanley earns 15¢ profit on each comic book. They can divide $19.50 by 15¢ to find the number of comic books he must buy and sell (130). Other students may want to make a table:

Number of comics	1	2	3	4	5	6	...
Profit	15¢	30¢	45¢	60¢	75¢	90¢	...

PROBLEM 160   Jonathan placed 10 pennies in a row on his desk. He replaced every other coin with a nickel. Then he replaced every third coin with a dime. What was the value of the 10 coins on his desk now?

Discussion   Act it out. Give the students coins or chips, or, simulate the action with pencil and paper. (See Figure B–27.)

Figure B–27

PROBLEM 161   Lucy has a dog, a parrot, a goldfish, and a Siamese cat. Their names are Lou, Dotty, Rover, and Sam. The parrot talks to Rover and Dotty. Sam cannot walk or fly. Rover runs away from the dog. What is the name of each of Lucy's pets?

Discussion   Prepare a logic matrix as shown. As each clue is given, record the information on the matrix. The first clue, "The parrot talks to Rover and Dotty," tells us that the parrot cannot be Rover or Dotty. Place X in the appropriate boxes in the matrix. The second clue, "Sam cannot walk or fly," tells us that Sam is the goldfish. Put a checkmark in the appropriate box and X's in all the remaining boxes in the Sam-goldfish row and column. Continuing this process establishes that the parrot is Lou, the dog is Dotty, the goldfish is Sam, and the cat is Rover.

	Dog	Parrot	Goldfish	Cat
Lou			x	
Dotty		x	x	
Rover		x	x	
Sam	x	x	✔	x

PROBLEM 162   Mary brought home a large pizza that had been cut into 8 equal slices. Her brother ate $\frac{1}{4}$ of the pizza as soon as she arrived home. Then her father ate $\frac{1}{2}$ of the rest of the pizza. Mary ate the rest. How many slices did Mary eat?

Discussion   For some students, manipulatives may be in order. Others may be able to simulate the action with a paper and pencil.

$$\frac{1}{4} \text{ of a pizza} = 2 \text{ slices}$$
$$8 - 2 = 6 \text{ slices}$$
$$\frac{1}{2} \text{ of 6 slices} = 3 \text{ slices}$$

Mary ate the remaining 3 slices.

PROBLEM 163   Farmer Grey plans to make a fence with 6 posts and some rope. One foot of rope will go around the first post, and 5 feet will be used to reach the next post. Another foot of rope will go around the post, 5 feet will be used to reach the next post, and so on. If the pattern continues to the last post, how many feet of rope does he need in all?

Discussion   Simulate the action with a drawing. There are 6 posts and 5 intervals, or sections of rope. Thus he needs $6 \times 1 + 5 \times 5$ or $6 + 25 = 31$ feet of rope.

PROBLEM 164   The 5 tags shown in Figure B–28 are placed in a bag. Stuart draws 3 of the tags out. His score is the sum of the numbers on the 3 tags drawn. How many different scores are possible and what are they?

$$\textcircled{5} \quad \textcircled{0} \quad \textcircled{2} \quad \textcircled{5} \quad \textcircled{7}$$

Figure B–28

Discussion   Make a table of all the possible scores. Notice that several scores repeat and should only be counted once.

5	5	0	7	2	Sum
x	x	x			10
x	x		x		17
x	x			x	12
x		x	x		12
x		x		x	7
x			x	x	14
	x	x	x		12
	x	x		x	7
	x		x	x	14
	x	x	x		9

There are only 6 different scores: 7, 9, 10, 12, 14, and 17.

PROBLEM 165 Mitch and his sister Pauline went to visit a friend who lives 12 blocks away. They walked 6 blocks when they realized that they had dropped a book. They walked back and found the book. Then they walked the 8 blocks to their friends house. How far from their home did they drop the book?

Discussion Some children will draw a diagram to illustrate the action in the problem. However, what is really needed is to subtract from the 12-block trip the 8 blocks they walked after finding the book. They dropped the book 4 blocks from their home.

PROBLEM 166 The Parents' Organization is holding its annual raffle to raise money for next year's field trips. How many tickets must they sell to pay for the 8 prizes?

BIG RAFFLE TONIGHT!!!		
	First Prize	$1,000
2	Second Prizes	$500 each
5	Third Prizes	$250 each
Tickets are $1.50 each.		

Discussion Divide and conquer. The students must first find out how much will be given away in prize money, namely $3,250. Dividing by the cost of one ticket, $1.50, yields an answer of 2,166.66. This must be interpreted as 2,167 tickets.

PROBLEM 167 My license tag is a 3-digit number. The product of the digits is 216; their sum is 19, and the digits appear in ascending order. Find my license plate number.

Discussion   Make a list of all the numbers whose product is 216 and which are single digits. There are only 3 such triples:

3, 8, 9—the sum of these is 20
4, 6, 9—the sum of these is 19
6, 6, 6—the sum of these is 18

Only 4, 6, and 9 satisfy the given conditions. The license plate number is 469. Note that this problem also provides a considerable amount of practice in factors, multiplication, and division.

PROBLEM 168   Sandra owes Charlene $1.35. Sandra and Charlene agree to split equally the cost of a $2 comic book. Sandra pays the $2 for the book. How much does Sandra now owe Charlene?

Discussion   Act it out or think it through. Sandra paid $2 for the comic book. Thus, Charlene's share was $1, which was paid by Sandra. Since Sandra owed Charlene $1.35, she now owes her only 35¢.

PROBLEM 169   In Figure B–29, how would you get 5 liters?

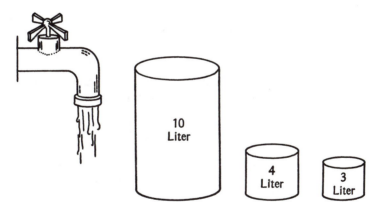

Figure B–29

Discussion   There are several ways to do this. For example,

(a) Fill the 10-liter pail and pour it into the 4-liter pail. This leaves 6 liters. Empty the 4-liter pail and fill it again from the 6 liters that remain in the 10-liter pail. There are now 2 liters in that pail. Now fill the 3-liter pail and pour the 3 liters into the 10-liter pail. There are now 5 liters in that pail.

(b) Fill the 4-liter pail and pour it into the 3-liter pail. This leaves 1 liter in the 4-liter pail, which should be poured into the 10-liter pail. Now refill the 4-liter pail and add those 4 liters to the 1 liter in the 10-liter pail, making 5 liters in all.

Ask your students to find additional ways.

PROBLEM 170   Complete the pattern:

$$
\begin{array}{rcl}
3 & \longrightarrow & 3 \\
26 & \longrightarrow & 8 \\
37 & \longrightarrow & 10 \\
18 & \longrightarrow & 9 \\
62 & \longrightarrow & 8 \\
49 & \longrightarrow & ? \\
31 & \longrightarrow & ?
\end{array}
$$

Discussion   This pattern may not be easy to see. However, the output is the sum of the digits of the input number. Thus, the missing outputs are 13 (4 + 9) and 4 (3 + 1). It is interesting for the students to notice that both 62 and 26 give an output of 8.

PROBLEM 171   July has 5 Tuesdays. Three of them fall on even-numbered dates. What is the date of the third Tuesday in July?

Discussion   July has 31 days. In order to have 5 Tuesdays, they would fall on one of the following sets of dates:

1	2	3
8	9	10
15	16	17
22	23	24
29	30	31

Since 3 of the dates must fall on even-numbered dates, the Tuesdays would fall on the 2nd, 9th, 16th, 23rd, and 30th. The third Tuesday in July would be July 16th.

PROBLEM 172   Shaun has just received a carton that contains 9 boxes of T-shirts. Unfortunately, rainwater wiped out the final digit on the invoice sheet (shown below). How many T-shirts did Shaun receive in this order of 9 boxes?

2,13 ?

200

Discussion   This is a problem for which the calculator comes in handy. Students can try dividing the numbers 2 130, 2 131, 2 132, 2 133 . . . by 9, until they arrive at a quotient with no remainder. Of course, if the students know that the sum of the digits must be divisible by 9 if the number is to be divisible by 9, then the problem can be solved without the use of a calculator.

PROBLEM 173   The 6 students in Mrs. Charnes' biology class were arranged numerically around a hexagonal lab table. What number student was opposite student number 4?

Discussion   Draw a diagram showing the 6 students around the hexagonal table. Number 1 is opposite number 4.

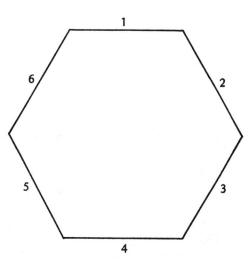

Figure B–30

PROBLEM 174   Club members are saving to buy records. The records cost $5 each. The club treasurer puts money into an envelope until the envelope has exactly $5 in it, then she starts another envelope. The members of the club have saved $37 so far. How many envelopes do they have?

Discussion   This problem can be acted out with chips, tokens, and envelopes. However, it can be done with an understanding of the meaning of division and remainders, an important concept. If we divide 5 into 37, we get a quotient of 7 and a remainder of 2. However, this remainder requires an envelope. Thus the club members have 8 envelopes.

PROBLEM 175   I am taking these people to dinner:

(a) me
(b) my wife
(c) my 2 sons and their wives
(d) each son's 2 children

How large a reservation should I make?

Discussion   Here is an opportunity to make a tree drawing (See Figure B–31).

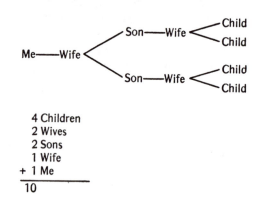

4 Children
2 Wives
2 Sons
1 Wife
+ 1 Me
_____
10

Figure B–31

I must make a reservation for 10 people.

PROBLEM 176   If 1 pound of plums contains 4 to 6 plums, what is the least possible weight in pounds of 3 dozen plums?

Discussion   Since a pound will contain 4, 5, or 6 plums, 3 dozen plums (36 plums) will weigh 9 pounds, $7\frac{1}{5}$ pounds, or 6 pounds. The least possible weight is 6 pounds.

PROBLEM 177   Mrs. Silvestri was driving along when she noticed that the number on the odometer of her new car read the same forward and backward. How many numbers like this are there between 100 and 1,000?

Discussion   Numbers that read the same backward and forward are called palindromes. Between 100 and 1,000 there are 90 palindromes. They can be found with a table:

101 111 121 131 141 151 161 171 181 191 (10 numbers)
202 212 222 232 242 252 262 272 282 292 (10 numbers)
303 313 323 333 343 ...   (10 numbers)

and so on. Thus, there are 9 groups of 10, or 90 such numbers.

PROBLEM 178   In January our team won 2 games and lost the same number. In February, the team lost 3 more games than it did in January, but won the same number of games it lost. In March, it won the same number of games as it did in February, but lost 2 fewer games than it did in February. What was its record at the end of March?

Discussion   Although the problem sounds complicated, organizing the data with a table *as you read it*, will simplify it.

	January	February	March	Total
Win	2	5	5	12
Lose	2	5	3	10

The team's record was 12 wins and 10 losses at the end of March.

PROBLEM 179   Ursula is in training. She did 5 sit-ups on the first day. She did 6 sit-ups on the second day, 7 on the third day, and so on. How many sit-ups did she do on the fourteenth day? On which day did she do 27 sit-ups?

Discussion   Write out 14 counting numbers beginning with 5. She did 5 sit-ups on the first day, 6 on the second day, 7 on the third day, 8 on the fourth day, ... She did 18 on the fourteenth day. Students should notice that the number of sit-ups is 4 more than the number of the day. Thus, she did 27 sit-ups on the twenty-third day.

PROBLEM 180   In Figure B–32, how many paths are there from Start to Finish?

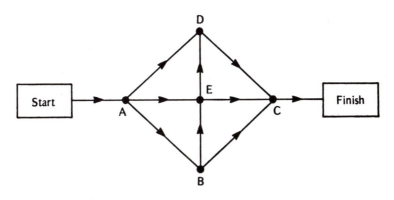

Figure B–32

Discussion   Make an exhaustive list of all the possibilities. Organize the list beginning with A-B.

Start-A-B-C-F   Start-A-D-C-F   Start-A-E-C-F
Start-A-B-E-C-F   Start-A-E-D-C-F
Start-A-B-E-D-C-F

There are 6 different paths from Start to F (finish).

PROBLEM 181   Jimmy is doing his laundry. He needs 4 quarters for each of the 5 loads he has to do. The change machine is broken and Jimmy forgot to bring any quarters. He notices that the machine that sells detergent takes a one-dollar bill and delivers a small box of detergent and 3 quarters in change. How many boxes of detergent will Jimmy have to buy to get enough change to wash his laundry? How many quarters will he have left?

Discussion   Make a table:

Boxes	Quarters (in change)
1	3
2	6
3	9
4	12
5	15
6	18
7	21

He must buy 7 boxes of detergent and he will have 1 quarter left (he needs 20 quarters for the 5 loads of laundry). Some students will simply divide 20 (the number of quarters he needs) by 3 (the number of quarters returned with each box of detergent), and round the quotient $6\frac{2}{3}$ to 7.

PROBLEM 182   A spider wishes to crawl from point H to point B (see Figure B–33). How many different "trips" can he crawl if each trip is exactly three edges long?

Discussion   Simulate the trips with pencil and paper, and make a record of the paths covered:

H-E-F-B   H-G-C-B   H-D-A-B
H-E-A-B   H-G-F-B   H-D-C-B

There are 6 possible trips the spider can take.

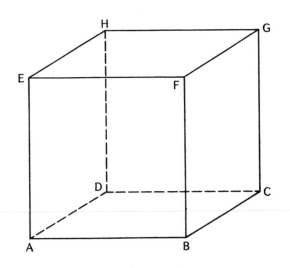

Figure B–33

PROBLEM 183   Theresa and Tony's mother just went to the hospital to have a new baby. "Boy," said Tony, "if it's a girl, I'll have twice as many sisters as brothers." "Yes," said Theresa," but if it is a girl, I'll have exactly the same number of sisters as brothers." How many children does their mother now have?

Discussion   Use guess and test. Their mother has 6 children now, 3 boys and 3 girls. If the baby is a girl, Tony will have 2 brothers and 4 sisters, twice as many sisters as brothers. If it's a girl, Theresa will have 3 sisters and 3 brothers, the same number of each.

PROBLEM 184   Last Saturday, George and his friend Mike went to a big-league baseball game. After the game, they went to the locker room to collect autographs of their favorite players. Together they collected 18 autographs, but Mike collected 4 more than George. How many autographs did George collect?

Discussion   Although this problem in an algebra class would provide a classic example of the simultaneous solution of 2 linear equations, it also provides an excellent opportunity for younger students to practice guess and test in conjunction with organized listing. A series of carefully chosen, recorded guesses adding to 18 leads to the numbers 11 and 7.

George	Mike	Total	Difference
0	18	18	18
1	17	18	16
2	16	18	14
3	15	18	12
.	.	.	.
.	.	.	.

George collected 7 autographs.

PROBLEM 185

In Graphtown, any street whose name begins with a vowel runs east-west, unless it also ends in a vowel, in which case it runs north-south. All the other streets can go either way. Berkeley Street runs perpendicular to Olive Street. In which direction does Berkeley Street run?

Discussion

Olive Street both begins and ends with a vowel. Therefore it must run north-south. Since Berkeley Street runs *perpendicular* to Olive Street, it must run east-west. Some students will have to draw a picture in order to see the action.

PROBLEM 186

Graphtown has intersections formed by 27 streets that run north-south and 31 streets that run east-west. If they plan to put 1 traffic light at each intersection of these streets, how many traffic lights will they need?

Discussion

The most direct way of dealing with this problem would be to actually draw the 31-line by 27-line grid and count the intersections. However, the complexity of the numbers can be reduced to a 2 × 2 grid, then a 2 × 3 grid, then a 2 × 4 grid, a 3 × 3 grid, etc. until we see that the product of the 2 numbers gives the number of intersections.

PROBLEM 187

Two owners of a pet shop agree to divide a tank of Siamese fighting fish. Mr. Jones took 72 of the fish. Mr. Smith took 92 of the fish and paid Mr. Jones $35. What is the value of 1 fish?

Discussion

There were a total of 72 + 92 = 164 fish in the tank. To divide them equally, each person would get 82 fish. Thus, Mr. Jones gave 10 of his 82 fish to Mr. Smith for $35. Each fish is worth $35 ÷ 10 or $3.50.

PROBLEM 188   Luisa was playing darts. She threw 3 darts, and all 3 hit the target shown in Figure B–34. Which of the following could be her score?

4,   17,   56,   28,   29,   31

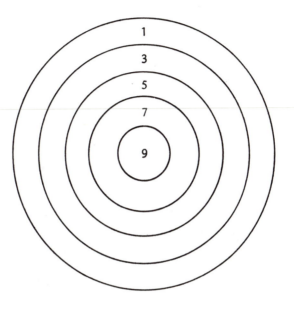

Figure B–34

Discussion   Since all 3 darts hit the target, Luisa's highest possible score could only be 3 × 9 or 27; similarly, her lowest score would be 3 × 1 or 3. Furthermore, since there are only odd numbers on the target, the 3 hits must give an odd sum. Thus, only 17 is a possible score for Luisa. She could have scored 17 in several ways:

$$9 + 5 + 3 = 17$$
$$7 + 5 + 5 = 17$$

PROBLEM 189   How many 2's must you multiply together to reach a 3-digit number?

Discussion   Use a calculator. Continue multiplying by 2 until you go from 64 to 128. There will be seven 2's.

PROBLEM 190   The Cartoon Video Company is making a videotape of cartoons for sale. They are using a tape that can run for exactly 3 hours. Each cartoon they are taping runs for either 30 minutes or 45 minutes. How many ways can they completely fill the tape?

207

Discussion   Make a table.

45 minutes	30 minutes
4	0
3	No
2	3
1	No
0	6

There are 3 ways to fill the tape.

PROBLEM 191   Sharon paints faces on Dilly Dolly dolls in the factory. She receives $5 for each large doll she paints and $2 for each small doll she paints. One day last week she received $18 for her work. How many of each size doll did she paint?

Discussion   Guess and test. She might have painted 9 small dolls and 0 large ones, or 4 small dolls and 2 large ones.

PROBLEM 192   Jeremy worked a math problem for homework last night and got 16 as his answer. However, in the last step he multiplied by 2 instead of dividing by 2. What should have been the correct answer?

Discussion   Work backwards. If Jeremy multiplied by 2 in his last step, he must have had 8 prior to that. If he had correctly divided by 2, then he would have gotten 4, the correct answer.

PROBLEM 193   Mr. Miller is putting up a post-and-rail fence along his property line. He uses 12 posts, approximately 8 feet apart. If he uses 2 rails between each 2 posts, about how many feet of railing should he buy? If posts cost $3.75 each and rails cost $2.50 each, how much will it cost Mr. Miller to put up the fence?

Discussion   Make a drawing to simulate the situation and determine the number of sections. Then divide and conquer. There are 12 posts, which will define 11 sections of rail. Since he uses 2 rails for each section, he will need 22 rails. Each is approximately 8 feet long, so he will need approximately 176 feet.

$$12 \text{ posts} \times \$3.75 \text{ per post} = \$45.00$$
$$22 \text{ rails} \times \$2.50 \text{ per rail} = \$55.00$$

His total cost will be $100.00.

PROBLEM 194   Mr. Baker has an order for 50 blueberry muffins. He has 2 sizes of muffin pans; one makes 8 muffins, the other makes 6 muffins. What is the smallest number of muffin pans he must use to make the 50 muffins?

Discussion   This problem can be solved by guess and test. Students might also decide to use manipulatives. Either of these methods will lead to the answer 4 pans of 8 muffins and 3 pans of 6 muffins for a total of 50 muffins. However, notice that Mr. Baker can use 7 pans of 8 to provide him with the required 50 muffins (of course, he will have 6 left over). He could also use 6 pans of 8 + 1 pan of 6, 5 pans of 8 + 2 pans of 6, and so on. Notice that in these latter 3 cases, he would not fill up all the pans if he wanted exactly 50 muffins.

PROBLEM 195   Jesse was looking at the cars in the dealer's lot and noticed that the cars were either red, white, or blue. Every white car in the lot had a black roof. Half of the blue cars had black roofs. Half of all of the cars with black roofs were white. There were 20 blue cars and 15 white ones. How many cars with black roofs were red?

Discussion   Every white car had a black roof, and there were 15 white cars. This establishes 15 cars with black roofs. Half of the blue cars have black roofs, and there are 20 blue cars. This establishes 10 more cars with black roofs, a total of 25. Half of all the cars with black roofs were white, so we know that there are 30 cars with black roofs. Therefore, 5 of them must be red cars with black roofs.

PROBLEM 196   Tanya and her older brother, Wilson, were discussing their ages. "Last year," said Wilson, "my age was a perfect square. Next year it will be a perfect cube." what is Wilson's age? How old will he be when his age is both a perfect square *and* a perfect cube?

Discussion   Make two lists, one of the perfect squares and one of the perfect cubes.

Squares	1	4	9	16	25	36	49	64	81
Cubes	1	8	27	64	125				

Since the problem refers to "last year" and "next year," we need two numbers that are 2 apart, namely 25 and 27. Thus, Wilson is currently 26 years old. The table reveals that only 64 is both a perfect square *and* a perfect cube (except for 1, which does not fit the rest of the problem conditions).

PROBLEM 197   Suzanne makes bracelets from sea shells. Claire, who is just starting to work at the shop, asked, "Suzanne, how much did you make during the first week you worked?" "Let's see, said Suzanne, "I've been working here for 6 weeks and I've made $15 more each week. This week I made $205." How much did she make the first week?

Discussion   Work backwards. Start with the sixth week. Suzanne earned $205. This is $15 more than she earned in the fifth week; thus she earned $190 during the fifth week. During the fourth week she earned $175; during the third week she earned $160; during the second week she earned $135; during the first week she earned $120.

PROBLEM 198   Johanna wants to record some rock and roll songs on a 30-minute audio tape she has just purchased. All of the songs will be either $2\frac{1}{2}$ minutes or 3 minutes in length. In what ways can she record the songs so that she completely fills the tape?

Discussion   Make a table like the one shown. The only 3 ways to completely fill up the tape are as shown. She can record 10 songs that are 3 minutes long; she can record 5 at 3 minutes and 6 at $2\frac{1}{2}$ minutes; or she can record 12 at $2\frac{1}{2}$ minutes.

3 min.	$2\frac{1}{2}$ min.	Full?
10	0	Yes
9	1	No
8	2	No
7	3	No
6	4	No
5	6	Yes
4	7	No
3	8	No
2	9	No
1	10	No
0	12	Yes

PROBLEM 199   Paula bought 20 comic books at 5 for $9. She then sold them all at $2 each. How much profit did she make?

Discussion   Do this problem by the divide and conquer strategy. Work each part separately. If she bought 20 comic books at 5 for $9, then she bought 4 × 5 books at 4 × $9 or $36. She then sold all 20 comic books for $2 each, receiving $40. Her profit was $40 − $36 = $4.

PROBLEM 200   Andrew had test scores of 88, 75, and 82 on his first 3 math tests. What is the lowest score he can get on the next test and still have an average of 80?

Discussion   In order to have an average of 80 on 4 test scores, his scores must total 4 × 80 or 320. He already has a total of 245. Therefore, the minimum score he can get is 75.

PROBLEM 201   On the last math test, the 10 students in Mr. Grace's math class had an average of 75. However, Mr. Grace failed to see a problem that Sam had done correctly. As a result, when he re-marked Sam's paper, Sam's grade went up by 20 points. How did this affect the class average?

Discussion   Use your knowledge of averages. Ten children with a class average of 75 means that the total number of points is 10 × 75 or 750. Sam's new score makes this 770. Dividing by 10 gives a new class average of 77. The class average went up by 2 points. Another approach would be to reason that, since Sam's score increased by 20 points and there were 10 students, the class average would go up by 20 ÷ 10 or 2 points.

PROBLEM 202   Four people enter a clubroom. Each person shakes hands with each of the other people. How many handshakes are there?

Discussion   You can act out the problem. Select 4 students and have them shake hands while the class keeps count, or make an exhaustive list:

A Shakes	B Shakes	C Shakes	D Shakes
A–B	B–A	C–A	D–A
A–C	B–C	C–B	D–B
A–D	B–D	C–D	D–C

Notice that several of the handshakes are the same. That is, if A shakes hands with B, that is the same as B shaking hands with A. Thus, repeats have been crossed out on the list. There will be 3 + 2 + 1 or 6 handshakes.

PROBLEM 203

See Figure B–35. Stephanie is going to spin each wheel. She will add the 2 numbers that result to get her score. What is the probability that the sum of the 2 selected numbers is even?

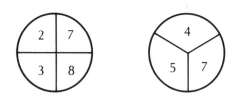

Figure B–35

Discussion

There are 12 possible scores. Have the children write them all out and count the number of even ones. There are exactly 6. Note: Since there are 2 even numbers and 2 odd numbers on the first wheel, whatever number occurs on the second wheel will produce the same number of odd sums as even sums.

PROBLEM 204

The 3-digit number $53A$ is exactly divisible by 6. Find the value of A.

Discussion

To be exactly divisible by 6, a number must be divisible by 2 (an even number) and divisible by 3. If we try $A = 0, 2, 4, 6$, or 8, we see that A must be 4. Thus $534 \div 6 = 89$. A more direct procedure would be to use the division algorithm, replacing the third digit with 0. Then $530 \div 6 = 88$ with a remainder of 2. But the remainder must be a 0 or a 6. Thus we need $A = 0 + 4$ or 4. The number is again 534.

PROBLEM 205

At what time, on a digital clock, does the sum of the digits show a maximum? When is it a minimum?

Discussion

When the students use guess and test, their initial reaction is to give an answer of 12:59 as the maximum. However, that digit sum is only 17. The maximum sum occurs at 9:59, for a digit sum of 23. The minimum sum occurs at 1:00, for a sum of 1.

PROBLEM 206   The drawing in Figure B–36 consists of alternating light and dark squares. How many more dark squares than light ones are there ?

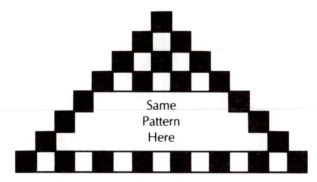

Figure B–36

Discussion   The pattern for the dark squares, beginning at the top, is 1 + 2 + 3 + 4 + 5 + 6 + 7 + 8 = 36. The pattern for the light squares begins in the second row and consists of 1 + 2 + 3 + 4 + 5 + 6 + 7 = 28. There are 8 more dark squares than light ones.

PROBLEM 207   Tom, Dick, and Henry were hired by the BioTech Company to paint a warehouse. Tom received $200 for his work. Dick received $65 for each room he painted. Henry received $18 an hour. They each painted 3 rooms and worked for 11 hours. Who earned the most money?

Discussion   Make an organized list.

        Henry: 11 hours × $18 per hour = $198
        Dick :   3 rooms × $65 per room = $195
        Tom :   = $200

Tom earned the most money.

PROBLEM 208   When Mr. Ravitz drives with his family from Florida all the way to Maine, he tries to entertain himself by keeping track of how far apart the signposts are along the way. How far apart are the two signposts shown in Figure B–37?

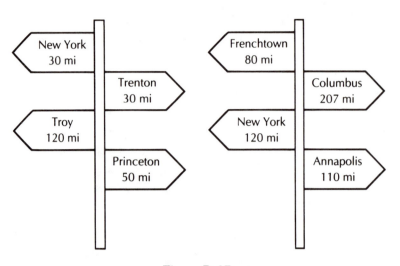

Figure B–37

Discussion   Students must find a city that occurs on both signposts. In this case, the city in question is New York. Since it is 120 miles away on 1 signpost and 30 miles away on the other, Mr. Ravitz has covered 90 miles from one signpost to the other.

PROBLEM 209   The students in Mr. Edwards' class collected $5.29 to give a gift to their teacher. Each student gave the same 5 coins. How many children are in the class? How much did each give?

Discussion   Use a calculator. Try to find the integral factors of 529. Students will find that 529 has exactly two sets of factors: 529 × 1 and 23 × 23. It is hardly likely that the class contains 1 student or 529 students. Thus, there are 23 students in the class, and each gave 23¢. (The 5 coins would be 2 dimes and 3 pennies.)

PROBLEM 210   Each player is to toss 3 beanbags at the target shown in Figure B–38. Janet hit 1 in B and 1 in C for a score of 52. Her third beanbag missed. Storm hit 1 in A and 1 in B for a score of 40. Dawn hit 1 in A and 1 in C for a score of 48. Cara hit 1 in A, 1 in B, and 1 in C. Find her score.

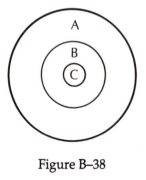

Figure B–38

Discussion   The total hits by Janet, Storm, and Dawn contain two A's, two B's and two C's. Thus we can add:

$$
\begin{array}{rcl}
B + C & = & 52 \\
A + B & = & 40 \\
A + C & = & 48 \\
\hline
2A + 2B + 2C & = & 140 \\
A + B + C & = & 70
\end{array}
$$

So Cara's score was 70.

PROBLEM 211   The areas of the faces of the box shown in Figure B–39 are given. What are the dimensions of the box?

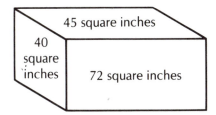

Figure B–39

Discussion   This problem can be solved by guess and test. Start with one face, the 45 square inches. The possibilities are 1 × 45, 3 × 15, and 5 × 9. Now take an adjacent face, 40. The possibilities here are 1 × 40, 2 × 20, 4 × 10, and 5 × 8. Thus, the common edge for these two faces must be 5. We find that the dimensions of the remaining face must be 8 × 9, so the box is 5 × 8 × 9.

PROBLEM 212   Jan forgot her lunch for school today but her friends brought theirs. Roz brought 3 sandwiches, and Gerry brought 5 sandwiches. The 3 girls decide to share the sandwiches equally, and Jan has $2.40 to pay for her share. How much should each of the other 2 girls receive from Jan?

Discussion   Since there are 8 sandwiches and 3 girls, each girl will have $8 \div 3$ or $2\frac{2}{3}$ sandwiches. Roz has 3 sandwiches ($\frac{9}{3}$) she will give Jan $\frac{1}{3}$ of a sandwich. Gerry has 5 sandwiches ($\frac{15}{3}$); she will give Jan $\frac{7}{3}$. The 2 girls will share the $2.40 in the ratio of 7:1. Roz gets 30¢, Gerry gets $2.10.

PROBLEM 213   The three killer whales at the Seaquarium weigh a total of 3,200 pounds. The baby whale weighs $\frac{1}{4}$ of the weight of the daddy whale. The mommy whale weighs 400 pounds less than the daddy whale. How much does each whale weigh?

Discussion   Guess and test. The baby whale weighs 400 pounds, the mommy whale weighs 1,200 pounds, and the daddy whale weighs 1,600 pounds. Students with some basic algebra skills can solve the problem with an equation:

$$x = \text{the weight of the baby whale}$$
$$4x = \text{the weight of the daddy whale}$$
$$4x - 400 = \text{the weight of the mommy whale}$$
$$(4x) + (4x - 400) + x = 3,200$$

PROBLEM 214   A mathematician was recently asked if he remembered the number on the basketball player's shirt. He replied, "I don't remember the number, but I do recall that it was a 2-digit perfect square and it had exactly 7 factors." What was the number?

Discussion   Since the number must be a perfect square with two digits, we try 16, 25, 36, 49, 64, and 81. The only one with exactly seven factors is 64.

PROBLEM 215   A blank video tape is marked for different recording times at different recording speeds as follows:

SP = 2 hours   LP = 4 hours   EP = 6 hours

Joe recorded a $1\frac{1}{2}$-hour show at the fastest speed (SP), then switched to the slowest speed (EP) and finished the tape. How long did he tape at the slowest speed?

Discussion   If Joe taped for $1\frac{1}{2}$ hours at the fastest speed (SP), he used up $\frac{3}{4}$ of the tape. Thus, at the slowest speed, he has $\frac{1}{4}$ of the tape left, or $(\frac{1}{4})(6) = 1\frac{1}{2}$ hours of additional time.

A Bibliography of Reasoning and Problem-Solving Resources

Arithmetic Teacher. The entire November 1977 and February 1982 issues are devoted to problem solving. National Council of Teachers of Mathematics, Reston, Virginia.

Barnard, Douglas. *A Book of Mathematical and Reasoning Problems.* D. Van Nostrand Company, New York, 1962.

Bransford, John D., and Stein, Barry S. The *Ideal Problem Solver.* W.H. Freeman and Company, San Francisco, 1984.

Brown, Stephen I., and Walter, Marion I. The *Art of Problem Posing.* Lawrence Erlbaum Associates, Hillsdale, New Jersey, 1990.

Butts, Thomas. *Problem Solving in Mathematics.* Scott Foresman and Company, Glenview, Illinois, 1973.

Curriculum and Evaluation Standards for School Mathematics. National Council of Teachers of Mathematics, Reston, Virginia, 1989.

Davidson, Patricia S., and Wilcutt, Robert E. *Spatial Problem Solving with Cuisenaire Rods.* Cuisenaire Corporation, New Rochelle, New York, 1985.

Dodson, J. *Characteristics of Successful Insightful Problem Solvers.* University Microfilm, Number 71–13, 048, Ann Arbor, Michigan, 1970.

Dolan, Daniel T., and Williamson, James. *Teaching Problem Solving Strategies.* Addison-Wesley Publishing Company, Menlo Park, California, 1983.

Enrichment for the Grades (27th Yearbook of N.C.T.M.). National Council of Teachers of Mathematics, Reston, Virginia, 1966–1971.

Fixx, James. *Games for the Superintelligent.* Doubleday and Company, Garden City, New York, 1972.

Gardner, Martin. *Aha!* Scientific American/W.H. Freeman and Company, San Francisco, 1978.

_____. *Gotcha!* Scientific American/W.H. Freeman and Company, San Francisco, 1982.

Greenes, Carol; Gregory, John; and Seymour, Dale. *Successful Problem Solving Techniques.* Creative Publications, Inc., Palo Alto, California, 1978.

_____; Spungin, Rika; and Dombrowski, Justine M. *Problem-Matics.* Creative Publications, Inc., Palo Alto, California, 1981.

Haynes, John R. *The Complete Problem Solver.* Franklin Institute Press, Philadelphia, 1981.

Hess, Adrien L., and Andersen, Lyle E. *Mathematics Project Handbook.* National Council of Teachers of Mathematics, Reston, Virginia, 1989.

Hill, Warren, and Edwards, Ronald. *Building Thinking Skills.* Midwest Publications, Pacific Grove, California, 1987.

Hirsch, Thomas L., and Wylie, C. Ray. *The Problem Pockets —Critical Thinking Activities.* Creative Publications, Inc., Palo Alto, California, 1986.

Holden, Linda. *Thinker Tasks: Critical Thinking Activities.* Creative Publications, Inc., Palo Alto, California, 1986.

Hyde, Arthur A., and Hyde, Pamela R. *Mathwise: Teaching Mathematical Thinking and Problem Solving.* Heinemann Educational Books, Portsmouth, New Hampshire, 1991.

Krulik, Stephen, and Rudnick, Jesse A. *A Sourcebook for Teaching Problem Solving.* Allyn and Bacon, Newton, Massachusetts, 1984.

_____. *Problem Solving: A Handbook for* Teachers (2nd ed.) Allyn and Bacon, Newton, Massachusetts, 1990.

_____. *Problem Solving in Math* (Levels G and H). Scholastic Book Services, New York, 1982.

Lenchner, George. *Creative Problem Solving in School Mathematics*. Houghton Mifflin, Inc., Boston, 1983.

Longley-Cook, L.H. *New Math Puzzle Book*. Van Nostrand Reinhold Company, New York, 1970.

May, Francis B. *Introduction to Games of Strategy*. Allyn and Bacon, Newton, Massachusetts, 1970.

Mott-Smith, Geoffrey. *Mathematical Puzzles for Beginners and Enthusiasts* (2nd ed.). Dover Publishing Company, New York, 1954.

Mottershead, Lorraine. *Metamorphosis: A Source Book of Mathematical Discovery*. Dale Seymour Publications, Palo Alto, California, 1977.

Overholt, James L; Rincon, Jane B.; and Ryan, Constance A. *Math Problem Solving: Beginners Through Grade 3*. Allyn and Bacon, Newton, Massachusetts, 1985.

Pedersen, Jean J., and Armbruster, Franz. *A New Twist: Developing Arithmetic Skills Through Problem Solving*. Addison-Wesley Publishing Company, Menlo Park, California, 1979.

Picciotto, Henry. *Pentomino Activities*. Creative Publications, Inc., Palo Alto, California, 1986.

Polya, George. *How to Solve It*. Princeton University Press, Princeton, New Jersey, 1971.

_____. *Mathematical Discovery: On Understanding, Learning and Teaching Problem Solving* (2 volumes). John Wiley and Sons, New York, 1965.

_____, and Kilpatrick, Jeremy. *The Stanford Mathematics Problem Book*. Teachers College Press, New York, 1971.

Problem Solving in School Mathematics (1980 Yearbook of the N.C.T.M.). National Council of Teachers of Mathematics, Reston, Virginia, 1980.

Professional Standards for Teaching Mathematics. National Council of Teachers of Mathematics, Reston, Virginia, 1991.

Ranucci, Ernest. *Puzzles, Problems, Posers, and Pastimes* (3 volumes). Houghton Mifflin Company, Boston, 1972.

Salkind, Charles T. *The Contest Problem Book* (2 volumes). Mathematical Association of America, Washington, D.C., 1975.

School Science and Mathematics. The entire March 1978 issue is devoted to problem solving. School Science and Mathematics Association, Kalamazoo, Michigan.

Sheffield, Linda J. *Problem Solving in Math* (Levels C–F). Scholastic Book Services, New York, 1982.

Swartz, Robert J., and Perkins, D.N. *Teaching Thinking: Issues and Approaches*. Midwest Publications Inc., Pacific Grove, California, 1989.

Throop, Sara. *Problem Solving* (3 volumes). Gamco Industries, Big Spring, Texas, 1983.

Trigg, C.W. *Mathematical Quickies*. McGraw-Hill Book Company, New York, 1967.

Whimby, Arthur, and Lochhead, Jack. *Problem Solving and Comprehension*. Lawrence Erlbaum Associates, Hillsdale, New Jersey, 1986.

_____. *Beyond Problem Solving and Comprehension*. Lawrence Erlbaum Associates, Hillsdale, New Jersey, 1984.

Wickelgren, Wayne. *How To Solve Problems*. W.H. Freeman and Company, San Francisco, 1974.

Williams, J.D. *The Compleate Strategist* (revised ed.). McGraw-Hill Book Company, New York, 1965.

Wylie, C.R. *One Hundred Puzzles in Thought and Logic*. Dover Publishing Company, New York, 1957.

SECTION D

Masters for
Selected Problems
(Problem Cards)

Connect the numbers from 1 through 20, in order.

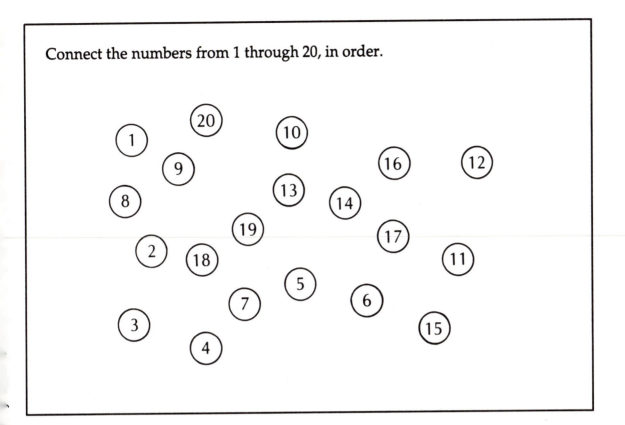

When I stand on my stilts my feet are as high as the top of my head when I am standing on the ground. The top of my head is 80 inches from the ground when I am standing on my stilts. How tall am I?

Amanda's grandfather gave her 6 nickels. She put them into her 3 piggy banks. How much did she put into each bank?

How many triangles whose vertices total 15 can you draw on the map below?

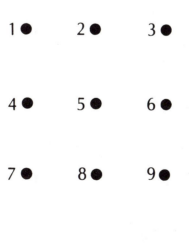

1●   2●   3●

4●   5●   6●

7●   8●   9●

Tom scored Tic-Tac-Toe, Three in a Row!! When he added the 3 numbers under his X's, he got a sum of 30. On what numbers did Tom's three X's fall?

8	12	14
6	10	5
9	13	11

Daniel, Michael, and Jeffrey made 13 baskets to be sold at the school crafts fair. Each boy made a different number of baskets, and no one made more than 6. Daniel made twice as many baskets as Michael. How many baskets did each boy make?

James has 3 banks. One is shaped like an elephant, one is shaped like a giraffe, and one is shaped like a turtle. Each bank has some nickels in it. There is 45¢ in all. We know the following facts:

1. The elephant bank is not empty.
2. The elephant bank has less in it than the giraffe bank.
3. The elephant bank has less in it than the turtle bank.
4. The turtle bank has less in it than the giraffe bank.

How much money is in each bank?

Each box has the same number of pencils inside How many pencils are in each box?

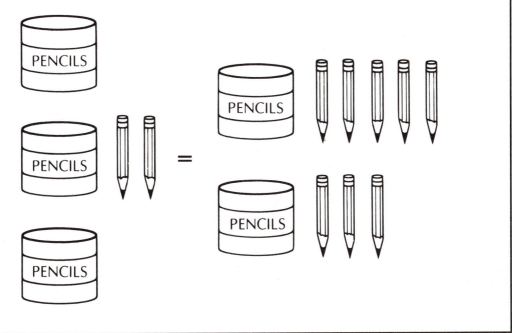

There is more than one coin in each of three banks. Banks A and B contain the same number of coins. Bank C has the most coins. If you multiply the number of coins in each bank together, the answer is 36. How many coins are in each bank?

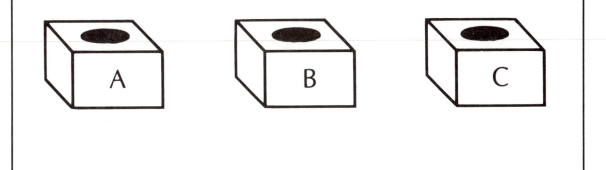

Glenda made a stack of cubes alongside her desk. She discovered that the stack contained an even number of cubes. Then she made two more stacks, each with the same number of cubes as her original stack. Was the total number of cubes in the stacks odd or even?

The new rock band, the Jumpin' Jeebies, is going to play in a school concert next Saturday night. The four members of the band are Jason, Jasmine, Jerome, and Jenine. Jerome and Jason have ears. Jerome does not have a nose. Jasmine and Jenine have hair. Jasmine has five blue spikes sticking out of the top of her head. What name goes with each picture?

(a)

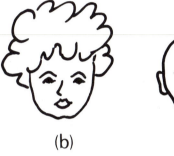

(b)

(c)

(d)

How much less does it cost a family of 2 adults and 3 children to visit the aquarium on a weekday than on a Saturday?

GRAND AQUARIUM OPENING!!!
SPECIAL PRICES

<u>Monday–Friday</u>
    Adults .... $ 4.50
    Children .... $ 2.25

<u>Saturday and Sunday</u>
    Adults .... $ 6.00
    Children .... $ 3.00

Elton brought a pizza to school, cut into equal-size pieces. He ate half of the slices and gave the rest to his three friends. Each of his friends received 2 slices. How many slices was the pizza been cut into?

A chicken can lay about 5 eggs each week. How many eggs can you expect 5 chickens to lay in 3 weeks?

Mrs. O'Brien has 3 children. Arlene is younger than Bonnie. Arlene is younger than Celeste. Bonnie is older than Celeste. The ages of the children are 6, 9, and 11. How old is Celeste?

My school is $\frac{1}{2}$ mile from my house. How many miles do I walk if I walk to school in the morning, walk home for lunch, and then walk home after school?

Maureen has $9. Beth has $5. Penny has $6. Lois has $4. Two of the girls put their money together and had a total of $9. Who were the 2 girls?

When Howard came to the bike rack, every slot was filled with a bike except the middle one, where he parked his bike. There were 8 bikes to the right of Howard's bike. How many bicycles are there in the rack?

Ann, Brad, Carol, and Daniel each wrote a report about a different kind of whale. Their reports were about blue whales, fin whales, humpbacks, and bowheads. Carol and Daniel did not write about humpbacks. Brad wrote about fin whales. Ann did not write about blue whales, and Daniel did not write about bowheads. Who wrote each report?

How far is the city from the state park? If you are halfway between the city and the state park, how far are you from the sign?

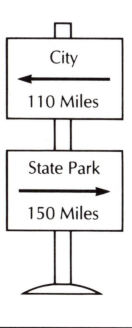

Nancy and Ellen each start reading a copy of *Gone with the Wind* on the first day of their summer vacation. Nancy decides to read 7 pages each day, but Ellen only wants to read 5 pages each day. When Nancy is on page 84, what page is Ellen reading?

The faces of a cube are numbered with consecutive numbers. Three faces of the cube are shown. Find the sum of the numbers on the faces of the cube.

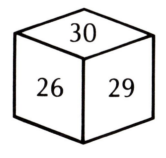

Peter, Paul and, Mary have 5 cookies. How many ways can they divide the cookies if each person must get at least 1 cookie and they do not break any of the cookies?

The record store has a sale on cassette tapes at $4, $5, $6, and $7 each. Lorraine bought some tapes and paid $12. What were the prices of the tapes Lorraine bought?

After finishing her shopping, Michele came home with $3.00. She had spent $3.25 on a present for her sister Beth, $4.25 for balloons for the party, and $5.00 for invitations. How much did Michele start with?

The houses on my street all have odd numbers. The first house is number 3, the second house is number 5, the third house is number 7, and so on. What is the number of the tenth house?

Helen works in a pet store. One of her jobs is to clean the canary cage each morning. Last Tuesday when she opened the door, half of them flew right out of the store. Of the ones that were left, 2 flew out of the cage and landed on the parrot cage, 5 landed on the tank that holds goldfish, and the remaining 8 flew into the room where the birdseed is stored. How many canaries were in the cage when Helen opened the door?

Rhoda, Sal, and Terry were scheduled to meet at the Town Hall at a certain time. The times at which they actually arrived were 11:05, 11:20, and 11:30. Rhoda arrived 5 minutes late. Sal arrived 10 minutes early, and Terry arrived 15 minutes late. At what time were they supposed to meet? At what time did each person arrive?

Jan and Marissa both swim at the local pool for exercise. They met each other while swimming on July 2. Marissa asked, "How often do you swim?" "I swim every third day, so my next workout will be on July 5," said Jan. "Well, I swim every fourth day, so my next workout will be on July 6," said Marissa. On what dates in July will the two girls both swim if they stick to their schedules?

Carl went running up to his teacher, all excited. "Look what I just discovered," he said. "When I open my math book to any page and add the page numbers on the two facing pages, I always get an odd number, but when I multiply them, I always get an even number." Is Carl right? If so, can you explain why it happens?

The new store in the mall opened last Saturday. As a promotional stunt, the store manager is giving a prize to every boy-girl pair that enters the store. Al, Benji, Charlie, Donna, and Evelyn are standing outside the store. Al turned to the others and said, "I wonder how many prizes we can get?" Donna answered," If we do it carefully we can get six prizes." Was Donna right? What was her thinking? How could they do it?

The score at the end of the eighth inning of the championship baseball game was 8–8. How many different scores were possible at the end of the seventh inning?

Louise is having a party. At lunch, they are seated around a circular table. A platter of 25 sandwiches is passed around the table, with each person taking one sandwich from the platter and passing it on to the next person. Louise takes the first sandwich and the last sandwich. How many people are seated at the table?

There are 20 children taking a hike through the Alaskan hills. They are walking single file through a pass. Two giant mosquitos at the other end have decided how they will bite the children. The first mosquito said, "I'll begin with the first one and then bite every third child (i.e., 1, 4, 7, 10, . . .)." The second mosquito said, "I'll begin with the second one and bite every other child (i.e., 2, 4, 6, . . .)." Which children get bitten twice? Which children don't get bitten at all?

The Carpenter family called up to order a pizza while they were watching the football game. "Cut it into 4 pieces," said Rusty, "and put mushrooms on all of it." " I want broccoli on half of it, said Mrs. Carpenter. "I want olives on half," said Mr. Carpenter. "And I want pepperoni on half, but not with the broccoli," said Susan. When the pizza arrived, all family members agreed that it was just what they had ordered. How were the toppings arranged on the pizza?

The hands on the clock shown are both the same size. How can you tell what time the clock really shows?

Giraffes walk in an unusual manner. On 1 step, they move their 2 right feet. On the next step, they move their 2 left feet. On the next step they move their 2 right feet, and so on. If a giraffe takes its first step with its 2 right feet, which feet will it move on the seventh step? Explain how you would decide which feet the giraffe moves on any step?

How many beads are on the string?

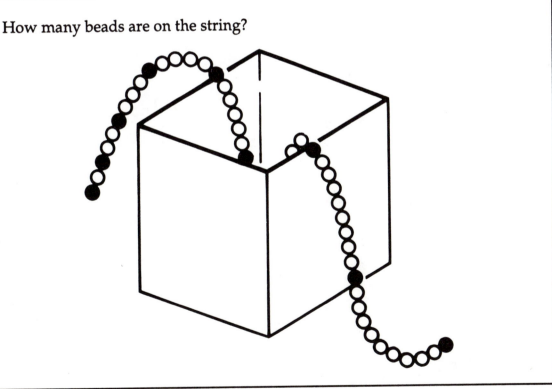

Mitchell just bought a new car. Lester said it was a blue Dodge. Patricia said it was a black Chevrolet. Sandy said it was a black Ford. If each person correctly identified either the make of the car or its color but not both, what was the actual color and make of Mitchell's new car?

A city block is about 270 feet long. Cars are parked bumper-to-bumper; a small car is 15 feet long, and a large car is 18 feet long.

(a) What is the smallest number of cars that can be parked in 1 block?
(b) What is the largest number of cars that can be parked in 1 block?
(c) If we park an equal number of large and small cars in 1 block, how many would fit?

On the new TV game show, each question is worth 3 times as much as the previous question. The fifth question on the show is worth $405. What is the first question worth?

Every night, Janet's dad puts all of his nickels, dimes, and quarters into a box. At the end of the month, he deposits the coins in the bank. Last month he deposited exactly $10. Janet noticed that he had the same number of nickels, dimes, and quarters. How many of each coin did her dad deposit in the bank?

Mrs. Miller wants to buy 27 prehistoric model figures so that she can give 1 to each student in her class. She can buy model dinosaurs that come 4 in a box, and she can buy the model cavemen singly. In how many different ways can she buy the 27 models?

At the fair, Janet and Mike were guessing how many corks were in a large jar. Mike guessed that there were 850 corks. The barker told him that he was off by 150 corks. Janet guessed that there were 1,100 corks in the jar. The barker told her that she, too, was off, but only by 100 corks. How many corks are in the jar?

One clock is 20 minutes fast. One clock is 15 minutes slow. One clock is 5 minutes fast. One clock is exactly right. What is the correct time?

On an assembly line that paints stripes around glass paperweights, there are 3 stations. The first station paints a red stripe on every third paperweight. The second station paints a green stripe on every fourth paperweight. The third station paints a blue stripe on every sixth paperweight. The machine produced 100 paperweights yesterday. How many of these had all 3 stripes on them?

The Clarks are planning a barbecue for the holiday weekend. They have invited 12 people. Morrie wants to serve the chicken at 6:30 P.M. The charcoal must burn for 20 to 30 minutes before he places the chickens on the grill. He plans to barbecue the chickens for 30 to 40 minutes before serving them. When should he start the charcoal?

Alim, Brenda, and Carol sold fruit at the school carnival. They sold oranges, apples, and pears.

(a) Alim and the orange seller are sisters.
(b) The apple seller is older than Brenda.
(c) Carol sold the pears.

Who sold each kind of fruit?

David has been raising tomatoes to sell at his roadside stand. He decides to put them into small baskets to sell. When he puts them into the baskets by 3's, he has 2 left over. When he puts them into the basket by 4's, he has 3 left over. If he knows that he has fewer than 100 tomatoes, how many might he have?

A triangular shape of grapefruit is placed on the window shelf in a local supermarket. The display is made by placing a row of grapefruit on the shelf and then a row containing 1 less grapefruit on top of that row. Continue in this way until 1 grapefruit is on the top row. If a total of 21 grapefruit are used, how many rows are in the triangular display?

Nicole has a package of silver stars. She wants to arrange them in rows, so that each row has the same number of stars. How can she arrange them so that the number of stars in each row is an odd number?

A farmer has 15 animals, some of them pigs and some chickens. Together they have a total of 40 legs. How many pigs and how many chickens does the farmer have?

Table of Moon Facts

The moon is smaller than the Earth.

People weigh 6 times as much on Earth as on the moon.

The moon goes around the Earth once every 28 days.

The moon is about 240,000 miles from Earth.

(a) Peter figures that he would weigh 14 pounds on the moon. What does Peter weigh on Earth?

(b) Peter's mother weighs 120 pounds on Earth. How much would she weigh on the moon?

(c) About how long does it take the moon to go around the Earth 4 times?

Half of the boys and girls who went to the fair ate ice cream. Half of the remaining girls ate popcorn. No boys ate popcorn. Altogether, 20 boys and 40 girls went to the fair. How many children ate neither ice cream nor popcorn?

A fancy bottle of perfume costs $25. The bottle alone without the perfume can be purchased by collectors. When purchased this way, the bottle alone costs $15 less than the perfume alone. How much does the bottle alone cost?

The Boy Scout troop earns money for charity by painting house numbers on the curb in front of each house. They receive 75¢ for each digit they paint. The house numbers begin with 1, then go up one number at a time: 2, 3, 4, ... When they were finished, they had earned $128.75. How many house numbers did they paint?

Mrs. Lewis bought 6 greeting cards. Mr. Lewis bought 6 cards that same day. How much would they have saved if they had bought the 12 cards together?

Number of Cards	1–3	4–4	7–9	10–12	13 or more
Cost for Each Card	$1.00	90¢	85¢	80¢	75¢

The big clock in the hall loses 5 minutes every hour. David set the clock at exactly 8:00 A.M. when he left for school. He came back at exactly 4:00 P.M. What time did the big clock show?

A rabbit ate 32 carrots in 4 days. If he ate 2 more carrots each day than he did the day before, how many carrots did he eat on each day?

Dan has a bad cold and has to take 1 teaspoon of cough syrup every $2\frac{1}{2}$ hours. He took his first dose at 9:00 A.M. He is supposed to take 6 doses before he goes to bed at 8:00 P.M. Can he do it?

The Forest Rangers are giving away 960 blue spruce saplings to be used in a reforestation project. The Jones Middle School is helping with the planting. They gave $\frac{1}{4}$ of the plants to the fifth grade class, and $\frac{1}{2}$ of that amount to the sixth grade class. The seventh grade class received $\frac{1}{2}$ of what was left, and the eighth grade class received $\frac{1}{4}$ of that number. They kept the plants that were left for next year's replacements. How many plants were left?

The cost of a concert ticket and a football ticket is $14. The cost of a movie ticket and a football ticket is $11. The cost of a concert ticket and a movie ticket is $7. Find the cost of each ticket.

At the record store, Carol bought the same number of tapes as records. She bought the same number of Western records as all the other records she bought. How many records and how many tapes did she buy if she bought 5 Western records?

Maureen brought an apple, an orange, and a peach to her science class. She weighed them 2 at a time. The apple and the orange weighed 14 ounces; the apple and the peach weighed 18 ounces; the orange and the peach weighed 18 ounces. How much did the apple weigh?

Mary bought a candy bar for 29¢. She gave the clerk a $1 bill and received 5 coins in change. What 5 coins did she receive?

Stanley makes extra money by buying and selling old comic books. He buys them for 85¢ each and sells them for $1.00 each. Stanley needs $19.50 to buy a new calculator. How many comic books must he buy and sell to earn the $19.50?

Jonathan placed 10 pennies in a row on his desk. He replaced every other coin with a nickel. Then he replaced every third coin with a dime. What was the value of the 10 coins on his desk now?

Lucy has a dog, a parrot, a goldfish, and a Siamese cat. Their names are Lou, Dotty, Rover, and Sam. The parrot talks to Rover and Dotty. Sam cannot walk or fly. Rover runs away from the dog. What is the name of each of Lucy's pets?

Mary brought home a large pizza that had been cut into 8 equal slices. Her brother ate $\frac{1}{4}$ of the pizza as soon as she got home. Then her father ate $\frac{1}{2}$ of the rest of the pizza. Mary ate the rest. How many slices did Mary eat?

Farmer Grey plans to make a fence with 6 posts and some rope. One foot of rope will go around the first post, and 5 feet will be used to reach the next post. Another foot of rope will go around the post, and 5 feet will be used to reach the next post, and so on. If the pattern continues to the last post, how many feet of rope does he need in all?

The five tags shown are placed in a bag. Stuart draws 3 of the tags out. His score is the sum of the numbers on the 3 tags drawn. How many different scores are possible, and what are they?

$$5 \quad 0 \quad 2 \quad 5 \quad 7$$

The Parents' Organization is holding its annual raffle to raise money for next year's field trips. How many tickets must they sell to pay for the 8 prizes?

BIG RAFFLE TONIGHT!!!	
First Prize	$1,000
2 Second Prizes	$500 each
5 Third Prizes	$250 each
Tickets are $1.50 each.	

Sandra owes Charlene $1.35. Sandra and Charlene agree to split equally the cost of a $2 comic book. Sandra pays the $2 for the book. How much does Sandra now owe Charlene?

Complete the pattern:

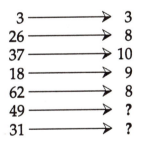

3 ⟶ 3
26 ⟶ 8
37 ⟶ 10
18 ⟶ 9
62 ⟶ 8
49 ⟶ ?
31 ⟶ ?

July has 5 Tuesdays. Three of them fall on even-numbered dates. What is the date of the third Tuesday in July?

Shaun has just received a carton that contains 9 boxes of T-shirts. Unfortunately, rainwater wiped out the final digit on the invoice sheet (shown below). How many T-shirts did Shaun receive in this order of 9 boxes?

2,13?

The 6 students in Mrs. Charnes' biology class were arranged numerically around a hexagonal lab table. What number student was opposite student number 4?

Club members are saving to buy records. The records cost $5 each. The club treasurer puts money into an envelope until the envelope has exactly $5 in it, then she starts another envelope. The members of the club have saved $37 so far. How many envelopes do they have?

If 1 pound of plums contains 4 to 6 plums, what is the least possible weight (in pounds) of 3 dozen plums?

Mrs. Silvestri was driving along when she noticed that the number on the odometer of her new car read the same forward and backward. How many numbers like this are there between 100 and 1,000 ?

Ursula is in training. She did 5 sit-ups on the first day. She did 6 sit-ups on the second day, 7 on the third day, and so on. How many sit-ups did she do on the fourteenth day? On which day did she do 27 sit-ups?

Jimmy is doing his laundry. He needs 4 quarters for each of the 5 loads he has to do. The change machine is broken and Jimmy forgot to bring any quarters. He notices that the machine that sells detergent takes a one-dollar bill and delivers a small box of detergent and 3 quarters in change. How many boxes of detergent will Jimmy have to buy to get enough change to wash his laundry? How many quarters will he have left?

Theresa's and Tony's mother just went to the hospital to have a new baby. "Boy," said Tony, "if it's a girl, I'll have twice as many sisters as brothers." "Yes," said Theresa, "but if it's a girl, I'll have exactly the same number of sisters and brothers." How many children does their mother now have?

Last Saturday, George and his friend Mike went to a big-league baseball game. After the game, they went to the locker room to collect autographs of their favorite players. Together they collected 18 autographs, but Mike collected 4 more than George. How many did George collect?

In Graphtown, any street whose name begins with a vowel runs east-west, unless it also ends in a vowel, in which case it runs north-south. All the other streets can go either way. Berkeley Street runs perpendicular to Olive Street. In which direction does Berkeley Street run?

Graphtown has intersections formed by 27 streets that run north-south and 31 streets that run east-west. If they plan to put one traffic light at each intersection of these streets, how many traffic lights will they need?

Two owners of a pet shop agree to divide a tank of Siamese fighting fish. Mr. Jones took 72 of the fish. Mr. Smith took 92 of the fish and paid Mr. Jones $35. What is the value of 1 fish?

Luisa was playing darts. She threw 3 darts, and all 3 hit the target shown. Which of the following could be her score?

4, 17, 56, 28, 29, 31

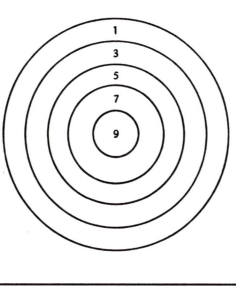

The Cartoon Video Company is making a videotape of cartoons for sale. They are using a tape that can run for exactly 3 hours. Each cartoon they are taping runs for either 30 minutes or 45 minutes. How many ways can they completely fill the tape?

Sharon paints faces on Dilly Dolly dolls in the factory. She receives $5 for each large doll she paints and $2 for each small doll she paints. One day last week she received $18 for her work. How many of each size did she paint?

Jeremy worked a math problem for homework last night and got 16 as his answer. However, in the last step he multiplied by 2 instead of dividing by 2. What should have been the correct answer?

Mr. Miller is putting up a post-and-rail fence along his property line. He uses 12 posts, approximately 8 feet apart. If he uses 2 rails between each 2 posts, about how many feet of railing should he buy? If posts cost $3.75 each and rails cost $2.50 each, how much will it cost Mr. Miller to put up the fence?

Mr. Baker has an order for 50 blueberry muffins. He has 2 sizes of muffin pans; one makes 8 muffins, the other makes 6 muffins. What is the smallest number of muffin pans he must use to make the 50 muffins?

Jesse was looking at the cars in the dealer's lot and noticed that the cars were either red, white, or blue. Every white car in the lot had a black roof. Half of the blue cars had black roofs. Half of all the cars with black roofs were white. There were 20 blue cars and 15 white ones. How many cars with black roofs were red?

Tanya and her older brother, Wilson, were discussing their ages. "Last year," said Wilson, "my age was a perfect square. Next year it will be a perfect cube." What is Wilson's age? How old will he be when his age is both a perfect square *and* a perfect cube?

Suzanne makes bracelets from sea shells. Claire, who is just starting to work at the shop, asked, "Suzanne, how much did you make during the first week you worked?" "Let's see," said Suzanne, "I've been working here for 6 weeks and I've made $15 more each week. This week I made $205." How much did she make during the first week?

Johanna wants to record some rock and roll songs on a 30-minute audio tape she has just purchased. All of the songs will be either $2\frac{1}{2}$ minutes or 3 minutes in length. In what ways can she record the songs so that she completely fills the tape?

Paula bought 20 comic books at 5 for $9. She then sold them all at $2 each. How much profit did she make?

Andrew had test scores of 88, 75, and 82 on his first 3 math tests. What is the lowest score he can get on the next test and still have an average of 80?

On the last math test, the 10 students in Mr. Grace's math class had an average of 75. However, Mr. Grace failed to see a problem that Sam had done correctly. As a result, when he re-marked Sam's paper, Sam's grade went up by 20 points. How did this affect the class average?

Stephanie is going to spin each wheel. She will add the 2 numbers that result to get her score. What is the probability that the sum of the 2 selected numbers is even?

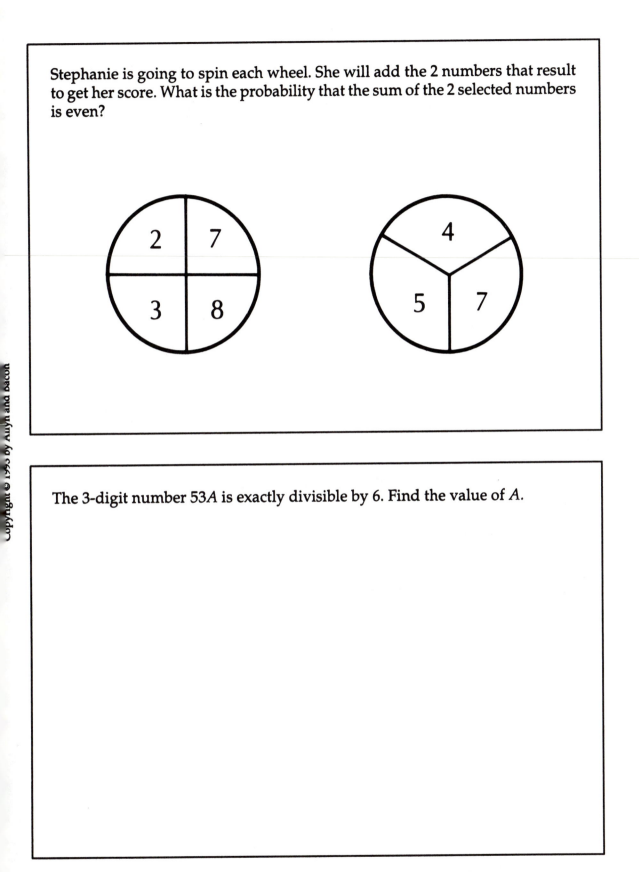

The 3-digit number 53A is exactly divisible by 6. Find the value of A.

At what time, on a digital clock, does the sum of the digits show a maximum? When is it a minimum?

The drawing shown consists of alternating light and dark squares. How many more dark squares than light ones are there?

Same
Pattern
Here

Tom, Dick, and Henry were hired by the BioTech Company to paint a warehouse. Tom received $200 for his work. Dick received $65 for each room he painted. Henry received $18 an hour. They each painted 3 rooms and worked for 11 hours. Who earned the most money?

When Mr. Ravitz drives with his family from Florida all the way to Maine, he tries to entertain himself by keeping track of how far apart the signposts are along the way. How far apart are the two signposts shown below?

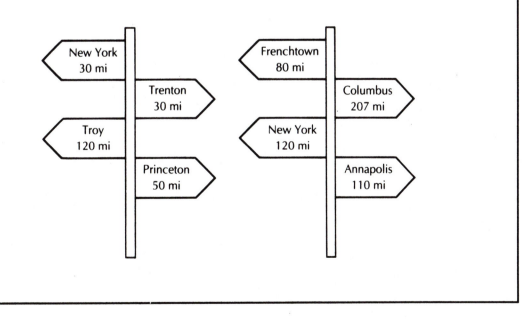

The students in Mr. Edwards' class collected $5.29 to give a gift to their teacher. Each student in the class gave the same 5 coins. How many children are in the class? How much did each give?

Each player is to toss 3 beanbags at the target shown. Janet hit 1 in B and 1 in C for a score of 52. Her third beanbag missed. Storm hit 1 in A and 1 in B for a score of 40. Dawn hit 1 in A and 1 in C for a score of 48. Cara hit 1 in A, 1 in B, and 1 in C. Find her score.

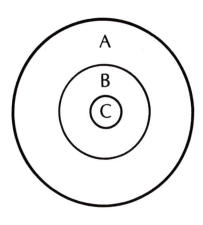

The areas of the faces of the box shown are given. What are the dimensions of the box?

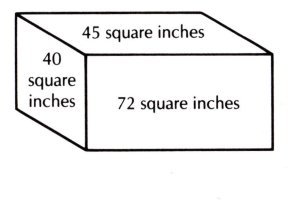

45 square inches

40 square inches

72 square inches

Jan forgot her lunch for school today, but her friends brought theirs. Roz brought 3 sandwiches, and Gerry brought 5 sandwiches. The 3 girls decided to share the sandwiches equally, and Jan has $2.40 to pay for her share. How much should each of the other 2 girls receive from Jan?

The three killer whales at the Seaquarium weigh a total of 3,200 pounds. The baby whale weighs $\frac{1}{4}$ of the weight of the daddy whale. The mommy whale weighs 400 pounds less than the daddy whale. How much does each whale weigh?

A mathematician was recently asked if he remembered the number on a basketball player's shirt. He replied, "I don't remember the number, but I do recall that it was a 2-digit perfect square and it had exactly 7 factors." What was the number?

A blank videotape is marked for different recording times at different recording speeds as follows:

SP = 2 hours   LP = 4 hours   EP = 6 hours

Joe recorded a $1\frac{1}{2}$-hour show at the fastest speed (SP), then switched to the slowest speed (EP) and finished the tape. How long did he tape at the slowest speed?

SECTION E

Masters for Selected Strategy Game Boards

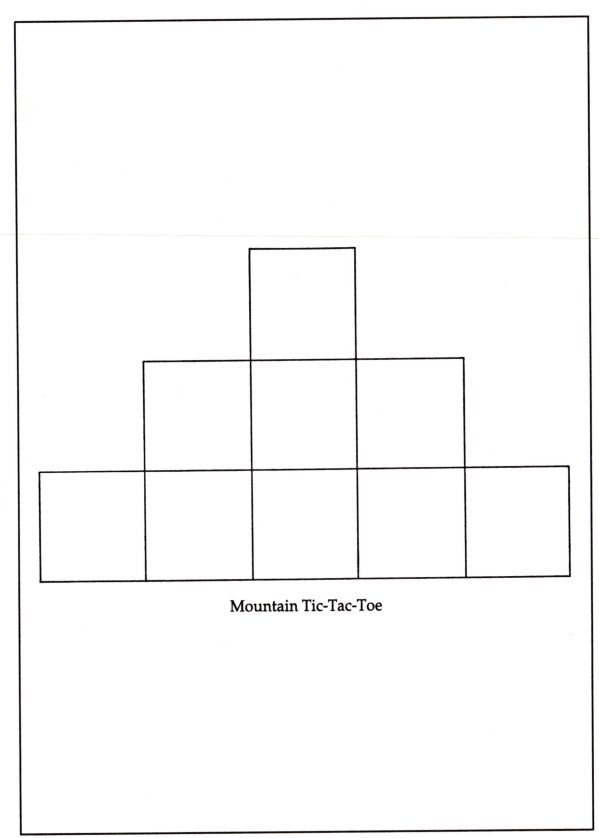

Mountain Tic-Tac-Toe

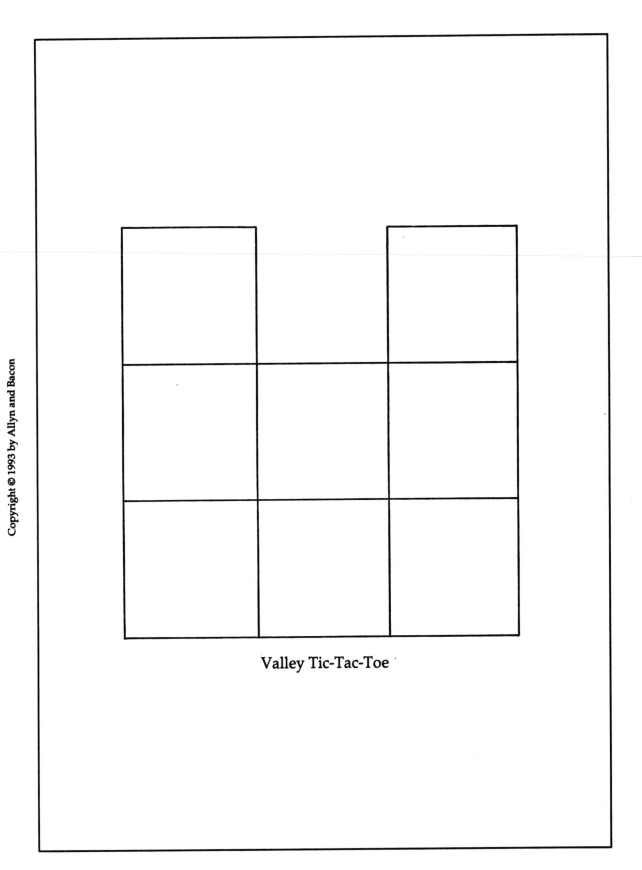

Valley Tic-Tac-Toe

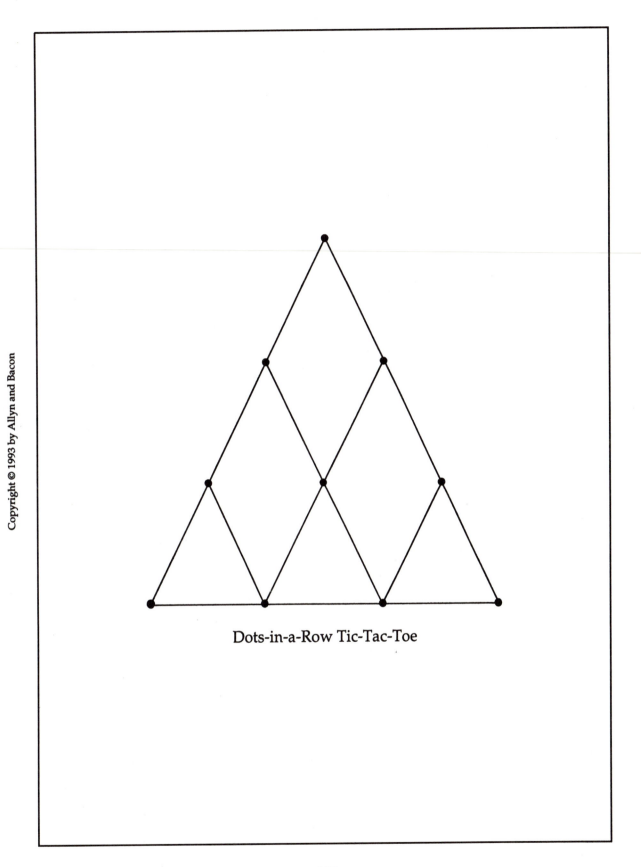

Dots-in-a-Row Tic-Tac-Toe

Tac-Tic-Toe

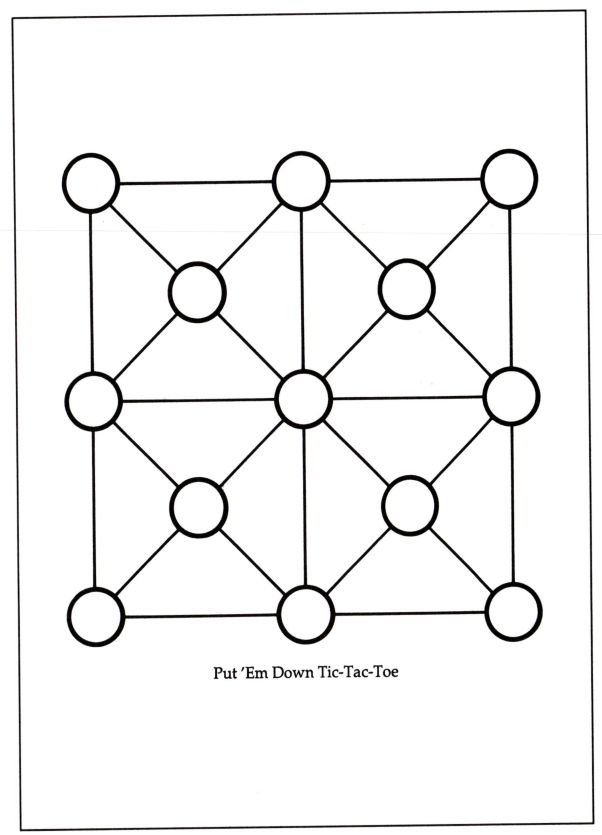

Put 'Em Down Tic-Tac-Toe

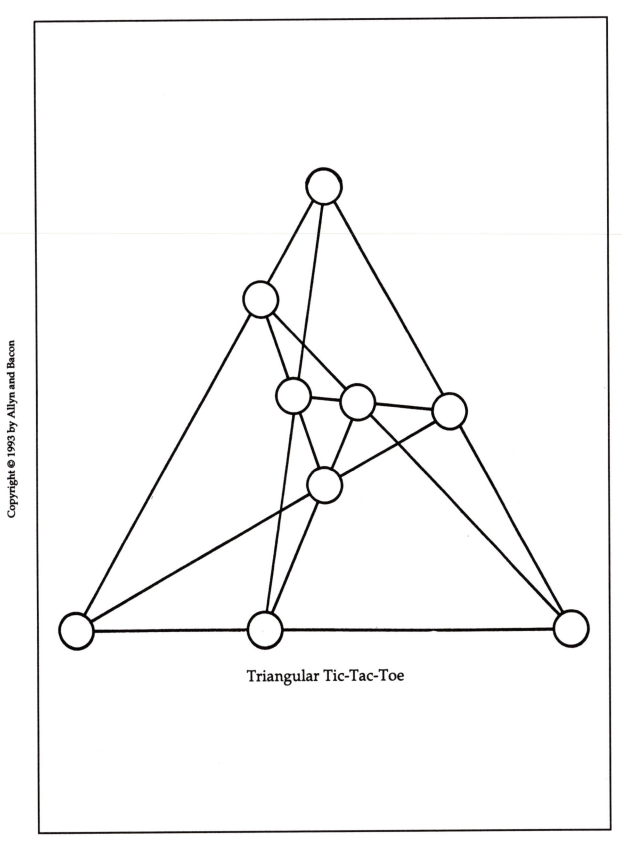

Triangular Tic-Tac-Toe

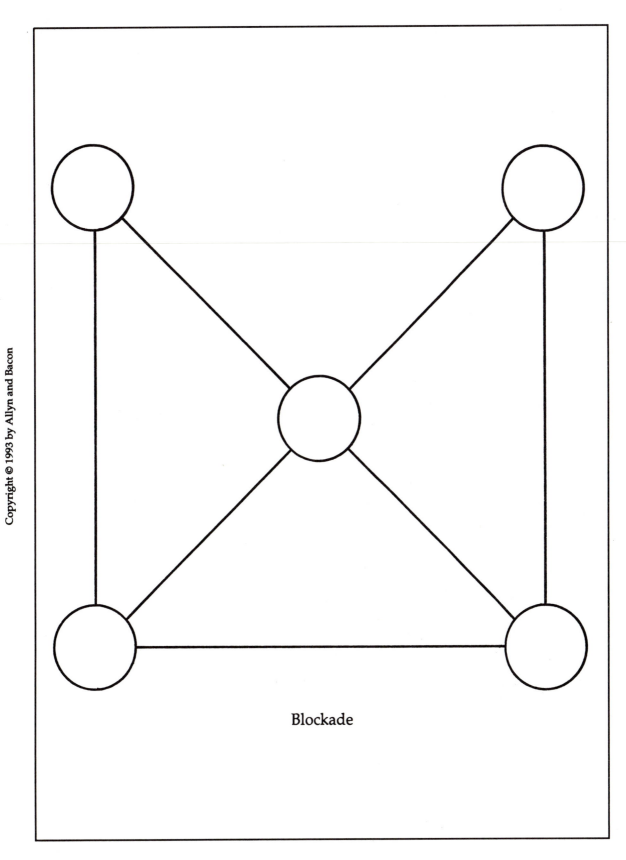

Blockade